Con Amore Mamma Agata

PAOLA

Mario

Gennaro

Mamma Agata
"Simple and genuine" Italian family recipes

For Brigitte,

from Mamma Agata

Ravello, June 2012

A very special thank you to Laura Faust (Ciao Laura) for assisting me in editing this book; Laura and I worked day and night between Nashville and Ravello translating the recipes, converting them into USA measurements, reading and re-reading the text, checking the grammar, and lastly, assisting me in expressing my feelings in proper English. Laura has been very precious for the realization of this book.

Thank you to Stephanie Bavaro for helping me with the recipes, the wording and for her great sense of humour and her positive attitude.

Thank you to ALL the people that helped me on this journey – including the photographers, the graphic artists and of course, my husband Gennaro to whom I dedicate this book!

THANK YOU

This has been really a LABOR of LOVE!

Editorial Director: Chiara Lima

Graphic design: Giulia Di Bartolomeo, white-studio.it
Photography:
Recipes Still life: Roberto Sammartini
Recipes steps: Michele Pappalardo
Reportages: Roberto Sammartini, Michele Pappalardo, Massimo Amendola, Alfonso Longobardi

Published in 2009 by Mamma Agata The Hidden Treasure Sas di Chiara Lima e C.
Reprinted in 2010, 2011.

Printed in Italy by EBS Editoriale Bortolazzi Stei - San Giovanni Lupatoto (Verona)

ISBN 978-88-904645-0-8

"Simple and genuine" Italian family recipes

To my parents for teaching me to love, share and work
with passion and honesty in everything that I do.

To my wonderful husband Gennaro for embracing all of my ideas
and being my support throughout this journey and of course
each day of our busy, happy life together.

To my beautiful children, Mario and Paola,
who are the joy and light of my life.

Chiara Lima

Contents

Windows in time   7

Tribute to Chiara Lima   8

The story of Mamma Agata's Life   11

The cooking school   21

The Hidden Treasure   27

Recipes   31

Sommelier Gennaro Petti   103

Meet papà Salvatore   165

Ravello   216

Windows *in time*

They say that life is made up of moments; moments that sharpen your senses and reinforce your vision and when your senses unite, you realize how fortunate you are to be in the moment, and recognize it for what it is – a window in time.

As you gaze over Mamma Agata's terrace that sits high up in the clouds in a jewel of a small Italian village of Ravello, the water surrounds your view and the air is clear and pure.
On the table before you are numerous little dishes holding secrets that taste like treasures. You'll find yourself nibbling on delicacies while listening to stories and engaging in colorful conversation.

Mamma Agata prepares a meal with love and respect. Agata has been cooking this way for most of her life. In fact, Mamma Agata was a mere teen when she began cooking in a local summer villa of a wealthy American woman who entertained many illustrious personalities in the 1950's and 1960's. At that time, Mamma Agata was known as "Baby Agata" since she was so young – young, but already a master of her craft of creating simple and elegant dishes.

Whether Mamma Agata is cooking for a large gathering or an impromptu poolside lunch, Mamma Agata's approach is always the same – she prepares traditional dishes with regional ingredients and Mamma Agata always remembers her guests' favorites. When Fred Astaire came to call after a lunch of "Pasta with zucchini and Eggplant Parmigiana," he was so overjoyed that he would Waltz around the courtyard with the hostess' elderly mother. Humphrey Bogart was more reserved, and he quietly ate a piece of Mamma Agata's Lemon cake while taking in the view.
The Pasta with Peppers and Sausage and Mamma Agata's meatballs were dishes exclusively reserved for Anita Eckberg, a gloriously tall woman with skin as creamy as milk. But my favorite memory that Mamma Agata shared with me is that of Jacqueline Kennedy who she said impressed her with "un eleganza molto simplice" - an elegant simplicity that was unique only to her and she loved to watch Mrs. Kennedy enjoy her "Spaghetti del contadino" as she lounged poolside.

Simple and Genuine. Two words that best explain the unique way in which Mamma Agata prepares and shares a meal at table.

Joan DiLieto

Tribute to *Chiara Lima*

If Mamma Agata is the soul of the family, Chiara is the heart.
She is the lifeblood, maintaining the 'heartbeat' of the household to ensure all parts work harmoniously. Through love and encouragement, Chiara constantly nourishes and provides support.

This description sounds like your conventional Southern Italian woman.
However, the urge to break the mould and be an independent woman of the world was evident from a young age. When she was 21, Chiara left home to study in Germany and a hospitality career spanning Germany, England, Switzerland and Ireland followed.
The youthful Chiara loved soaking up her new surroundings, fascinated by the kaleidoscope of people, food, customs and environments. Her newfound ability to bridge cultural divides by speaking different languages and broaden her knowledge in each country inspired Chiara tremendously.
Chiara's travels broadened her attitudes and mind-frame, reinforcing the importance of helping, appreciating and understanding others instilled in her as a child.

There is no doubt that Chiara is a 'people' person who genuinely loves to share her knowledge and life with others. One of the first things you will notice when you meet Chiara is her positive energy – her vivacity, a smile that lights up her entire face and the twinkle in her eye. The very same twinkle that Mamma Agata reveals when she recalls her wonderful youth at the villa. Chiara's generosity of spirit is evident when she welcomes you into her home and immediately treats you like a member of the family, fussing about like a mother and making sure you have the very best of everything! Her ability to laugh at herself and see the humour in all situations is the reason why Chiara is able to maintain her optimism and thriving business.

Chiara's inspiration, passion and determination come from her family (her grandmother in particular) and her travels. What is most admirable is her continual drive to learn, improve and deliver the very best in everything she does whilst keeping a smile on her face and never complaining. As a daughter, mother, wife and businesswoman, this is no mean feat and makes her a true 'hidden treasure'.

Kim Bate

The Story of Mamma Agata's *Life*

Welcome to the life story of Mamma Agata. My name is Chiara Lima. I am the youngest daughter of Agata Lima who is affectionately known as "Mamma Agata". As you will see, I will serve as the narrator throughout this book – and my hope is that you will walk with me through the story of our lives, just as you would walk through a garden – absorbing all of the wonderful aromas, colours and flavors along the way.

Our family is truly honoured you have made the decision to purchase our very first cookbook, and we hope you will enjoy reading about our lives, and share our passion for food, life and family traditions.

Talking about our lives in the first person is never an easy task, but so many of our guests have asked us to do so, and I am happy to finally be able to say that it is with much love that I am ready to share Mamma Agata's life story with you.

Our hope is to be able to share our deep and intense feelings, passion and love of cooking with you – whether you are cooking for yourself or for your friends and family – we hope that you do it with love because no matter what the occasion, we believe deeply that cooking is love!

So, back to the beginning – Mamma Agata was born Agata Amato on February 25, 1942 in the coastal village of Ravello, Italy. During that time, life in the region was harsh due to widespread poverty stemming from the aftermath of WWII.

Agata was born into a large Italian family of seven brothers and sisters. As with many large families, it was sometimes difficult to make ends meet. Thankfully, the Amato family was fortunate to own a small plot of land, a cow, a few hens and some rabbits, which made them luckier than most; however, times were tough. Agata learned from a very young age that in order to survive, she must work hard and remain strong. It was these trying times that shaped Agata into the effervescent person we know, love and cherish today.

The Story of Mamma Agata's Life

As a child, Mamma Agata learned to appreciate very basic values in life and she had a deep respect for the land and farm animals. She understood that the land yielded nutritious vegetables for the family, the cow provided fresh milk for the children, the hens produced eggs; and on very rare occasions such as holidays, the rabbits were celebrated for their prized meat.

In modern times, we think of these things as being so simple, yet they are such important elements in our daily existence. Agata never took anything for granted and this simplicity has followed her throughout her life and has become her "modo di vivere" which mean way of life in Italian. Mamma Agata still prepares each and every meal for her family today with the same special care that she takes when she is preparing food for a wedding or private dinner on our terrace and of course, for our beloved cooking school.

And so the story goes, Agata began cooking for her siblings and other family members at the very young age of 8, and as she grew into her adolescent years, her mother, grandmother and aunts would all chip in to teach Agata family recipes, tips and secrets of food preparation. While Agata didn't always succeed on her first try, her elders provided a voice for her inner strength and she learned to never give up – an attitude that remains deeply rooted within her soul.

Agata's knowledge and respect for food was one that she took very seriously - her parents instilled a generous spirit in her, which created a pattern in her life; with the little they had, they still shared meals with the less fortunate and they always gave back to the community.

As a young girl, Agata's chores included collecting herbs from the mountains and tending to the garden in Ravello. On occasion, the eggs from the family's hen were traded for flour and the rabbits were exchanged for clothes and shoes for the children. Once a month, they baked special breads of which one was soft and the other bread was a type of biscuit that would last for up to a month if necessary. As always, any leftovers were generously shared with the less fortunate townspeople.

The Story of Mamma Agata's Life

By the time Agata was in her adolescent years, she became an avid writer and she often had dreams of becoming a journalist; however, as fate would have it, her family could not afford to send her to upper level schools, so she began to write on her own and thankfully for us, Agata recorded family recipes in her journal.

Mamma Agata has always been a sponge for knowledge – especially when it comes to cooking! From a very early age, she has been on a never ending quest to absorb culinary tips and secrets whenever possible.

As Agata's curiosity and imagination progressed, she would begin to solicit nearby farmers to learn more about the process of tending land, inquire into the unique flavors of their herbs and of course, experiment on her own on how to incorporate these wonderful smells and flavors into her every day cooking. Agata also loved to talk to the local fisherman, who shared their secrets of fish stories with her, as well as their personal recipes to incorporate the many species of fish that can be found in the sea along the Amalfi Coast.

While her grandparents were still alive and well, Agata spent many hours with them, learning as much as possible. Many locals have said that her interest in the land, culture and regional cuisine was profound for someone so young. Lucky for us, Mamma Agata's knowledge in the kitchen is one of the treasures of a lifetime and is yet another layer added to our very special Hidden Treasure!

All of the tips that Agata absorbed proved to be quite helpful in launching her cooking career when she was only thirteen years old - something she did on her own in order to assist her parents in providing basic necessities of life to her family.

Villa Civita

Thankfully, fate was on her side and Agata's first employer was Marajen Stevick Chinigo, an American heiress who lived in Torre di Civita in Ravello. Ms. Chinigo enjoyed Agata's cooking so immensely that she hired her to serve as a private chef in her home

The Story of Mamma Agata's Life

— the now famous Villa Civita, a grand villa overlooking the sea in Ravello.

It wasn't long before Agata became a household name in the A-list Hollywood circles and it was not at all unusual for her to cook for Ms. Chirigo's famous guests who were famous American movie stars and politicians of the time. Needless to say, Agata's intuition in the kitchen was natural, and after a few months of preparing classic American cuisine, she persuaded her employers to shift to the regional specialties of our beloved Amalfi coast, which of course they loved!

During the time she was serving as Ms. Chirigo's personal chef, Humphrey Bogart gave her the name "Baby Agata" since she was so young. Mr. Bogart had a wonderful sense of humor and he loved Agata's now famous lemon cake — actually, once he got a taste of it, he simply refused to eat his breakfast without it! Mamma Agata also fondly remembers one of his other favorites - alici fritti (fried anchovies) which he would enjoy quietly on the patio in the afternoon while taking in the view.

Each morning, Ms. Chirigo and Baby Agata would plan their menu for the day, but it wasn't long before Agata earned her respect and faith and started making all the daily cooking and party menu decisions on her own.

My mother has so many little funny and sweet stories about her 15 year working with Ms. Chirigo, including her time spent at the villa and all of the famous Hollywood stars that she met throughout those years.

One of the most wonderful memories that my mother shared with me is that each Saturday evening, Ms. Chirigo would host the most magnificently grand cocktail parties that you could ever imagine; literally rivers of expensive French champagne flowed and the guests were also treated to the very best Russian caviar, and of course Agata's Simple and Genuine food. Guests always included famous actors and politicians of the time – and since Ms. Chirigo trusted Agata so much, she quickly became the person who handled all of the responsibilities of the gala dinners and parties that went well into the night – still a fond memory for Mamma Agata to this day!

Whether she was cooking for a large gathering or an impromptu poolside lunch, Agata's approach was always the same and one of her special gifts is that she always remembers her guest's favorite dishes. When Fred Astaire came to call on Ms. Chirigo, he would enjoy his favorite lunch and would waltz around the courtyard with her elderly mother. Agata would watch with delight, it was as if a cinema was coming to life in front of her very own eyes!

Mamma Agata has many fond memories from this time in her life, including preparing her family recipe of Pappardelle with peppers and sausage and meatballs for Anita Eckberg, who was a gloriously tall woman with creamy skin like the color of milk. But Mamma always told me that her favorite celebrity memory is that of Jacqueline Kennedy, who impressed her with "un'eleganza molto simplice" - a simple elegance that was uniquely her own. Agata was fascinated by Mrs. Kennedy and loved to watch her sit and enjoy a Caprese salad by the pool or a nice plate of Mamma's farmer spaghetti. She also adored watching little John-John eat her lemon cake with such joy and pleasure!

In addition to meeting the famous actors, artists and politicians of the time, Agata met the love of her life Salvatore. They married and were blessed with two daughters, my sister Giovanna and me, Chiara. Due to complications related to Giovanna's birth, Agata became quite ill and she almost lost her eyesight. Thankfully, her strong will and determination prevailed and she fully recovered and risked everything to have me (THANK GOD!).

Mamma Agata always wanted a big family, but her two pregnancies proved to be dangerous to her health. Feeling lucky to have 2 precious children, she concentrated on raising us, as well as looking after her elderly parents while working as a private chef to help support the rest of her family.

Mamma Agata was highly sought after to prepare private dinners for Italy's elite such as the Agnelli family. They always adored Mamma's fried pizza that she prepared for their gatherings, as well as her famous lemon cake. The lemon cake in particular quickly gained popularity within the elite circles. It became the perfect dessert to have at any party because of its simplicity and deliciousness.

As my sister and I grew older, it became important to my mother to be able to provide opportunities to us that she was unable to enjoy as a child. Mamma's will to provide a good life for us was so strong that she began selling her delicious cakes, limoncello liqueur and many different kinds of marmalades to vacationers staying in private villas.

Mamma Agata's sacrifices have always been grand, and it should come as no surprise to hear that she worked day and night in order to be able to send my sister and me to university. Mamma never complained, or shed a tear, and her positive attitude and faith carried her through more financial trials that lay ahead in the family's future.

"Never give up" and "where there is a will, there is a way" are important and cherished values that Mamma Agata instilled onto my sister and me.

The Story of Mamma Agata's Life

A journalist once wrote that Mamma Agata is a heroine because not only was she a forward thinking woman for her time, but she was also an exquisite chef and she set the bar high as an excellent role model for her family.

In fact, after the parties at Villa Civita, Agata asked for permission to take the leftovers to share with family, friends and others whom she barely knew, but was well aware that they were in need of nourishment. Mamma Agata was always more than happy to provide this help. Today our family's spirit of charity remains the same – we continue to distribute excess food after private dinners and weddings to those who need it more than we do.

Easter happens to be the most joyous time of year in our home; and we rejoice in the happiness of this giving season.

During Easter, Mamma Agata makes a classic Italian Pastiera Napoletana cake, an ancient tradition, and a cake that needs hours and hours of preparation time, since it contains more than 20 ingredients. This is a complex and tiring recipe to make, standing for many hours until every last cake has been completed. As the years have passed, and Mamma Agata has progressed in age, we now beg her to sit down and make

fewer cakes, but she simply will not hear of it!

She continues to make at least thirty cakes each Easter to distribute to friends, family, neighbors and to those who have lost their lifelong partners. Mamma also includes those who are along during the Easter Holiday and those who cannot afford such luxuries.

A deep love and passion for life, deliciously prepared foods, wonderful wines; each component plays an integral part of the world that we have created, and that we hope to share with you in Ravello at our Hidden Treasure!

As you read through the pages in this book, we hope you'll find our recipes to be *Simple and Genuine*; these two words really speak volumes about us – they truly express our way of life in the best possible sense of the words! And of course, we must include one more word that is very important to us – a word you may have already guessed by now - PASSION – the combination of these three words really complete the full description of our lives, love, respect for our culture and our cuisine!

Our entire family would welcome you with open arms in celebrating our love for a *Simple and Genuine* (and passionate!) way of life – cooking – friendship – land – culture – what is ours is yours and we would love you to visit us and share our passion as often as possible!

Thank you so much for listening to our story. It is very important for us to express and share our love with you through our recipes. We can't wait until you will try our dishes in the comfort of your very own home, where you can share the flavors of Mamma Agata with your family, friends and party guests alike to create an unforgettable meal where our *Simple and Genuine* recipes will transform a daily gathering into a true feast!

On behalf of Mamma Agata, myself and the rest of our dear family, we hope you will love your family and friends and leave all your problems behind you prepare your meals. Learn to enjoy the wonderful sounds of the tomato sauce bubbling on the stove top,

Mamma Agata

the splashing of the pasta as it jumps into the pan with the tomato sauce - even imagine the pasta as if it were enjoying the most luxurious bath of its life – then the addition of the fragrant herbs to further enhance your senses! Please remember, life is enhanced by the joy of being together and by sharing a special moment with your loved ones.

Our cooking philosophy is *Simple and Genuine*, whinch we hope to share and pass on through our first cookbook created just for you and with love.

With much love,

Chiara Lima, daughter of Mamma Agata

The Cooking School
With special thanks to our *Guardian Angel*

This is the story of the birth of the precious Hidden Treasure cooking school. As you'll see, this was simply a natural progression in the lives of Mamma Agata, me and the rest of our precious family.

Here is how it all began:
When I was just 21 years old, I had the urge to leave Ravello to broaden my horizons, explore new cultures and learn to speak foreign languages, so I set off and travelled abroad and did just that!

After nearly 6 years of travelling in Germany, England, Switzerland and Ireland, studying, making new friends and working in the tourism industry abroad, I realized that I was homesick and it was time to bring this worldly knowledge home with me to my beloved home in Ravello. I had finally realized that there really is no place like home, and I longed for the fragrant scents coming from Mamma Agata's kitchen – especially on Sunday mornings, when Mamma has her ragù meat sauce simmering for hours.

I missed the gorgeous, warm sunny days in Ravello, where the sun shines brightly on our home that is perched high on a cliff overlooking the sea. I also dearly missed the gardens and landscape of our family property – including waking to the smell of the fresh grass cut in the morning and the rich scents of the vine harvest each autumn.
Upon my return to Ravello, I decided to build my future in the hospitality business; however, when I arrived back home I quickly realized that my life in Ravello had changed and my parents needed me more than ever.

Mamma Agata told me not to worry while I was away and travelling, but upon my return, I found my father, Salvatore, struggling to maintain our large garden on his own – he often had to call workers to assist him with the lemon groves, digging deep wells in the soil to regenerate and rotate the plantation, and the olive and vine harvest was nearly impossible to do on his own and even with my mother's help, it

The Cooking School

the hidden treasure

was still too much work for two people.
I suddenly realized that the future of our family's property was in danger, and we had to find a way to step in and help our future generations so they would be given the opportunity to grow and live on the land that had been so good to us.

I thought back to the days of my youth, when I studied and learned to tend the garden with my father, and also the loving memories I had playing with my childhood friends, and small creatures that lived in the garden – such as frogs and lizards. I also remembered back to the days when I would cut the grass, prune the garden or just lie in the grass gazing at the sky, listening to the birds or simply looking out over the sea from our family home.

I knew in my heart that I absolutely had to find a way to rescue my family and our beloved property. I spent many long hours searching for ways to create something special out of these memories – to share them with visitors perhaps?

My days were long during this period of my life, as I needed to work outside of our home to support the family until we could figure out a way to bottle Mamma Agata's memories and create new ones for visitors close and far to cherish, just as she had always done.

One day, a little voice inside my head told me there was an obvious solution – and it was right in front of me the entire time! I could take Mamma Agata's skills in the kitchen, along with her history of cooking for some of the most important actors and politicians of her time – people such as Gore Vidal, Giovanni Agnelli, Humphrey Bogart Jacqueline Kennedy Onassis, and package it into a cooking school!

I know that the voice was my Guardian Angel who is my grandmother Chiara, she loved this family and this home as much as I do....and I KNOW she helped me to find the way to help everybody!

My Grandmother Chiara who is my precious Guardian Angel and my grandfather Pantaleone.

Mamma Agata

The Cooking School

After all, they all really loved her cooking and raved about it to all of their friends. And Mamma Agata's neighbors were always calling Mamma Agata for advice in the kitchen – so I had a sense that my mother's recipes would be huge hit with people who could only dream of tasting foods prepared freshly from fruits and vegetables in their garden.

I knew we had to find a way to share Mamma Agata's lemon cake, and her eggplant parmigiana, meatballs, pizza recipes with the rest of the world!

Well, that was it! It would be Mamma Agata's passion that could rescue the family, the land and at the same time, we would finally be able to share her secrets of *Simple and Genuine* cooking and share our love of Ravello with all those who would visit the Hidden Treasure and take interest in learning to cook with passion like Mamma Agata!

So, with the project in mind, in 1994 I began promoting the cooking school! But this was not easy as it is today – we had no computer and certainly no website and no means of purchasing one anytime soon - our Guardian Angel must have watching over us!

After many long hours of research and saving my money, I found a company based in the United Kingdom that would provide web service and create a website to promote our new business – Mamma Agata's Cooking School on the Amalfi Coast! It took another year before we would be able to afford a computer, so during this time I was only receiving correspondence via fax. Once we had full access to the internet, I was able to really start promoting our business around the world.

The Cooking School

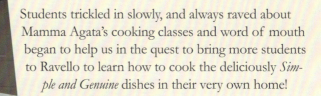

Students trickled in slowly, and always raved about Mamma Agata's cooking classes and word of mouth began to help us in the quest to bring more students to Ravello to learn how to cook the deliciously *Simple and Genuine* dishes in their very own home!

To this day, students continue to be amazed by the rich flavors created with such ease using simple ingredients from our land.

Suddenly, students were re-creating Mamma Agata's recipes around the world for their friends – and they began to wonder if their friends liked them for themselves or for their cooking!

Thanks again to our Guardian Angel, the cooking school began to do really well and the media soon picked up on the Hidden Treasure and cooking lessons provided by Mamma Agata and wrote lovely articles on the experience, on Mamma Agata's life history cooking for the famous actors and politicians and of course for the extreme passion she has for cooking.

Mamma Agata quickly became a legend along the Amalfi Coast and Ravello and numerous articles have been written on her life in such glamorous publications as Lexus Magazine, Elle Magazine, Cosmopolitan, Condè Nast Traveller, Food and Wine Magazine and many more.

The Cooking School

The property was rescued! And Mamma Agata's passion and giving spirit brings us so much joy and we love to share this with people from all over the world, making all of their lives that much happier and providing a sense of fulfillment and purpose in life.

Now we welcome students from all around the world – all nationalities, ages, reasons for celebrations such as honeymooners, birthdays and those seeking a beautifully romantic wedding experience on the patio. Each and every one of the visitors loves Mamma Agata, and my husband Gennaro who has become an integral part of our tightly woven family – as a professional Sommelier and a licensed cheese and olive oil tasting expert.

Our family was strong and has always had strong faith, and it was Mamma Agata who taught the family to never give up – and she took this advice literally and after a short period of time, my family and I envisioned using our natural resources and combined talents to create the cooking school that we know and love today.

It was a culmination of our family's hard work and commitment to maintain our property and well-being that this beloved Hidden Treasure was born! And of course, a little luck and oversight by our Guardian Angel too!

The *Hidden* Treasure

If you have even wondered why we call our cooking school *The Hidden Treasure*, well I will give you the answer. Upon sharing our secret with you, I hope you will agree with me that the name fits us perfectly!

One of the reasons we call Mamma Agata's cooking school *The Hidden Treasure* begins with a description of the property itself, which is situated approximately 1000 feet above sea level. The crowning jewel of the property is the physical building that houses Mamma Agata's cooking school and sits majestically at the top with a breathtaking view overlooking the Amalfi Coastline.

When you stand at the edge of the property and look down, you can see all of the beautiful green mountains. As your eyes continue along, they are met by the glorious blue sea with its wonderful colors and various shades of blue. At times, the blending is so perfect that it's difficult to determine where the sea ends and the sky begins.

The Hidden Treasure was actually established about 250 years ago when our family first arrived on the property. Mamma Agata, Salvatore, Gennaro and me, and our children Mario and Paola are the forth, fifth, and sixth generations of our family to inhabit this property.

About 250 years ago my great, great, great grandparents settled in this exact location and they built everything from scratch – the cisterns, the terraces with the vegetable gardens and even our house! There was literally nothing here, but they owned the property from the terrace all way down to the sea. Once they had children, the property was split and it continued to split as each of the children in the family had children and so on.

The Hidden Treasure

Now we have inherited the property and terraces about half way down to the sea; the rest of the property belongs to our cousins. In fact, our cousins are so close that when we run out of something, like sugar or olive oil, we simply call their names from the terraces rather than calling them on the telephone!

We feel that God has truly blessed Mamma Agata and our family, as we own a piece of property that has a great view of the sea and is easily accessible from the road, which makes it easy for our visitors to get it. The view from *The Hidden Treasure* is surreal as you experience a land suspended between the sea and the sky – a place some can only dream about and we are so fortunate to be able to share this with you!

From the moment you arrive and walk down the stairs from our entrance, you get the sense that you are entering into a little piece of heaven – a place so near the sky and the sea at the same time – a place that is surrounded by colourful flowers in shades of purple, pink, white, violet and bougainvillea vines overhead. And last but not least, the sweet smell of jasmine vine creates a grand, but subtle welcome into our little slice of heaven!

Two steps more and your eyes rise to the view of the ocean and your feel a sense of calmness and peace as you take in the view of the sea, and the silence is only interrupted by the birds singing or the bells of the cathedral ringing on the hour. Occasionally, you can even hear the sounds of sea gulls gawking or a territory battle between a hawk and a crow, or the one of the many frogs hopping around in the spring – *The Hidden Treasure* is a place where you can stop regenerate your spirit and hear your soul singing praises to you for finding such peace and tranquillity – even if only for just a short while.

The other reason we call our property *The Hidden Treasure* is because as legend goes, at the end of every rainbow one finds a pot of gold. Mamma Agata's cooking school is at the end of the rainbow and when you visit us, you will have found your Pot of Gold. Come join us at our Hidden Treasure.

Chiara Lima

Recipes

Pastella di Mamma Agata
BATTER FOR DIPPING AND FRYING

250 gr or 2 cups flour (Fine "00" flour or white pastry flour)
25 gr or 1 teaspoon sugar
100 gr or ¾ cup Parmigiano cheese (grated)
1 Egg
200 ml or 1 cup water (lukewarm/tepid)
25 gr or 1 ¾ Tablespoons baking yeast (dry or cake yeast fresh)
2 pinches of sea salt
2 teaspoons white vinegar

In a bowl, combine the flour, sugar and cheese (1, 2, 3).

Add the egg to the bowl and mix thoroughly (4).

In a separate smaller bowl, dissolve the yeast in the tepid water (5).

Add the water and yeast to the flour mixture until the consistency is similar to that of a thin pancake batter (6, 7). NOTE:
• If the batter is too thick, add a 1 or 2 tablespoons of water to thin it out.
• If the batter is too thin, add a little more flour to thicken it.

Mamma Agata's Recommendation:
The batter will be lumpy. Please do not try to dissolve the lumps. Be careful not to overwork the batter or the yeast will not rise. Do not use a food processor or electric mixer for this recipe.

Cover the bowl and set it aside in a warm, draft-free location for one hour. NOTE: Air conditioning and drafts can kill the yeast. Mamma Agata suggests placing the batter in a cool oven (i.e. one that is not turned on).

After one hour, the batter will have risen. Add the vinegar and salt to the batter and stir. NOTE: the batter will fall when stirred; this is normal.

COCKTAILS

The batter is now ready for use either as a dipping batter (with zucchini strips, shrimp, broccoli, etc.) or to make fritters (i.e. **Mamma Agata's Coccoli**) by adding ingredients into this mixture (salami, grated zucchini, minced onion, herbs, etc.).

Mamma Agata's Secrets

The water for yeast must be lukewarm/tepid to the touch. Water that is either too cold or too hot will kill the yeast and in the end, the batter will not rise.

Whenever you make a batter or dough with yeast, you must add sugar to activate the yeast. Without sugar, salt will kill the yeast and the batter/dough will not rise.

Mamma Agata uses very fine flour (type "00" in Italy) for all of her recipes. If you are not able to find "00" flour, you may use white pastry flour.

The reason we add vinegar to the batter is that it inhibits oil from penetrating the batter during the frying process.

Coccoli di Mamma Agata
MAMMA AGATA'S COCCOLI

Mamma Agata's Pastella (Batter)
½ onion (grated)
50 gr or 1 ¾ oz of bacon or salami (finely chopped)
1 tender/small zucchini (For this recipe you will use the skin ONLY, finely grated)
1 teaspoon rosemary (finely chopped)
1 teaspoon sage (finely chopped)
1 teaspoon thyme (finely chopped)
100 gr or ½ cup Parmigiano cheese (grated)
1 litre or 1 quart peanut or vegetable oil for frying (NOTE: Do not use olive oil)

Prepare **Mamma Agata's Pastella** (see page 32).

In a bowl, combine all of the above chopped/grated ingredients: onion, salami/bacon, zucchini skin, rosemary, sage, thyme and Parmigiano cheese.
Add all of the ingredients to the batter and mix well (1).

Follow **Mamma Agata's Frying Instructions** (see page 47).
Using a table spoon, gather a spoonful of Coccoli batter and add it to the hot oil (2). Do not overcrowd the pan or it will reduce the temperature of the oil and the Coccoli will absorb too much grease.

Mamma Agata's Secret
Keep a glass of water near the Coccoli batter to dip the spoon. The water will keep the batter from sticking to the spoon. You may need to dip the spoon several times during this process to keep it from sticking. Be careful to keep the water away from the frying oil.

Fry the Coccoli on each side for one to two minutes, until both sides turn a nice golden brown (3). Remove the Coccoli from the oil and place on paper towels to absorb excess oil.
Serve hot!

NOTE: This recipe is great for cocktail receptions, weddings, anniversaries and birthday parties - or any other special occasion where you need delicious finger food!

Involtini di melanzane
EGGPLANT ROLLS

2 eggplants (long, thin and firm, such as Japanese eggplants)
50 gr or 1 ¾ oz grated Parmigiano cheese (grated)
50 gr or 1 ¾ oz smoked Provolone or Gouda cheese (shaved)
20 arugula leaves
6 sun-dried tomatoes
Sea salt, as needed
1 litre or 1 quart peanut or vegetable oil for frying (NOTE: Do not use olive oil)
Wooden Toothpicks

Mamma Agata's Secrets
The type of eggplant that Mamma Agata uses is very important in this recipe. The eggplant needs to be long, thin and firm; Japanese eggplants work well. Ultimately, the shape, firmness and (low) water content are critical to the success of a good eggplant. Less water in the eggplants means more flavor in your dish and no soggy Eggplant Rolls!

Wash the eggplant and remove the top and end of each eggplant. Use a vegetable peeler to peel the skin of the eggplant lengthwise (i.e. along the length of the eggplant) in stripes, like a zebra, keeping some of the skin on the eggplant to preserve the essential vitamins and flavor of the eggplant.
Once the eggplant is peeled, slice the eggplant lengthwise into long pieces about ½ to 1-inch thick. Do not slice it too thin, as it will reduce in size during cooking.

Layer the eggplant slices around the edge of a colander/strainer; sprinkle each slice of eggplant with a pinch of sea salt. Allow the salted eggplant to sit for thirty minutes, to assist in draining out excess water and removing the bitter taste from the eggplant.

After thirty minutes, gently squeeze out excess water from the eggplant slices, 3-4 slices of eggplant at a time, starting from the top of the slices to the bottom. Do not rinse off the salt, eggplant is like a sponge and it will absorb the water. (NOTE: These ingredients and instructions are identical to the **Eggplant Parmigiana.** Please refer to the **Eggplant Parmigiana** recipe if that provides additional guidance).

Place the flour on a plate. Dip each slice of eggplant into the flour to cover on both sides (1). Work quickly, as you do not want the eggplant to absorb too much flour or they will become too soggy to fry.

Frying the Eggplant.

Follow **Mamma Agata's Frying Instructions** (see page 47) to fry the eggplant until they are golden brown (2). Remove the eggplant from the oil and place them onto a paper towel to absorb any excess oil (3).

Shave slices of the smoked Provolone or Gouda cheese. The cheese must be shaved very thinly so that it rolls easily within the eggplant.

Mamma Agata's Secret
You have to build the eggplant rolls while the eggplant is still very hot to melt the cheese, making it more compact and easier to roll.

Place the eggplant slices on a hard work surface, with a paper towel underneath each piece to allow the paper towel to continue absorbing excess oil (4). Sprinkle each slice of eggplant with Parmigiano cheese (4), Provolone cheese (5) and whatever else you like, such as a few arugula leaves (5).

Carefully roll each slice of eggplant (6) making sure to keep the ingredients intact as you roll them. Place a wooden toothpick through the middle of each eggplant roll to hold the ingredients in place.

Prepare additional eggplant rolls, always using Parmigiano and Provolone cheeses, plus any other ingredients you like in order to create new unique flavors. Other suggestions include sun-dried tomatoes (7), and bacon or smoked ham, all depending on our individual tastes. You may experiment with your favorite ingredients; just make sure they are very thinly sliced so that they roll easily within the eggplant slices.

These rolls are great to serve at a party – just slice the individual rolls into two pieces to create your own little Italian eggplant sushi rolls (8). Of course, the rolls make a wonderful appetizer to serve prior to any main course!

Fiori di zucchine imbottiti
Stuffed Zucchini Flowers

4 zucchini flowers
4 pieces of smoked Provolone or Gouda cheese (sliced)
Mamma Agata's Pastella (Batter)
1 litre or 1 quart peanut or vegetable oil for frying (NOTE: Do not use olive oil)

Prepare **Mamma Agata's Pastella** (see page 32).

Clean the zucchini flowers and remove the stems, keeping the rest of the flower intact (1).

Slice the smoked cheese into 3-inch strips – about ½ inch thick (2).

Stuff each zucchini flower with a strip of smoked cheese. Optionally, you may add bacon, salami or ham to the cheese (3).

Gently twist the tops of the flowers to seal in the ingredients. Be careful not to tear the flower, as the flower is delicate. It is very important to make sure the cheese is completely contained within the flower, so that it does not fall into the oil and ruin your batch of flowers.

Follow **Mamma Agata's Frying Instructions** (see page 47).

Dip the zucchini flowers into the batter and then gently place them into the pan to fry for two minutes on each side carefully flipping the flower when golden brown (4).

Remove the Zucchini Flowers from the oil and place on paper towels to absorb excess oil.

Serve hot!

NOTE: This recipe is great as a starter for formal or informal meals.

Parmigiana di melanzane
Eggplant Parmigiana

Serves 4
8 eggplants (long, thin and firm, such as Japanese eggplants)
Sea Salt
250 gr or 1/2 lb Mozzarella cheese
150 gr or 1 ½ cups Parmigiano/Parmesan cheese (grated)
100 gr or ½ lb smoked Provolone cheese (or any similar smoked cheese such as gouda)
50 gr or 1 ¾ oz "00" flour (or white pastry flour) to coat the eggplant
20 basil leaves
1 litre or 1 quart peanut or vegetable oil for frying (NOTE: Do not use olive oil)
1 cup of **Mamma Agata's Tomato Sauce**

Prepare **Mamma Agata's Tomato Sauce** (see page 55) and set aside.

Mamma Agata's Secrets
The type of eggplant that Mamma Agata uses is very important in this recipe. The eggplant needs to be long, thin and firm; Japanese eggplants work well. Ultimately, the shape, firmness and (low) water content is critical to the success of a good Eggplant Parmigiana (see the pictures in this recipe to get an idea of what is best). Less water in the eggplants means more flavor in your dish and no soggy Eggplant Parmigiana!

Buy fresh mozzarella cheese (in water) two days before making your Eggplant Parmigiana. Remove the cheese from the water and place in a covered bowl in the refrigerator to dry out. Otherwise, all of the water contained in the mozzarella will leak into your eggplant and you will have a soggy Eggplant Parmigiana.

Preparation of the Eggplant
Wash the eggplant and remove the top and end of each eggplant. Use a vegetable peeler to peel the skin of the eggplant lengthwise (i.e. along the length of the eggplant) in stripes, like a zebra, keeping some of the skin on the eggplant to preserve the essential vitamins and flavor of the eggplant (1).

Once the eggplant is peeled, slice the eggplant lengthwise into long pieces about ½ to 1-inch thick. Do not slice it too thin, as it will reduce in size during cooking (2).

Layer the eggplant slices around the edge of a colander/strainer and sprinkle each slice with a pinch of sea salt. Allow the salted eggplant to sit for thirty minutes to drain the excess water and remove the bitter taste (2).

After thirty minutes, gently squeeze out excess water from the eggplant slices, 3-4 slices of eggplant at a time, starting from the top of the slices to the bottom. Do not rinse off the salt, as eggplants are like sponges and they will absorb the water (3).

Place the flour on a plate. Dip each slice of eggplant into the flour to cover on both sides (4). Work quickly, as you do not want the eggplant to absorb too much flour or they will become too soggy to fry.

Frying the Eggplant
Follow **Mamma Agata's Frying Instructions** (see page 47) to fry the eggplants until they are golden brown. Remove the eggplant from the oil and place them onto a paper towel to absorb any excess oil (5, 6, 7).

Preparing the Eggplant Parmigiana

Pre-heat the oven to 150 degrees Celsius (325 degrees Fahrenheit).

Gather the ingredients, including **Mamma Agata's Tomato Sauce**, the sliced mozzarella and provolone cheeses, grated Parmigiano cheese, and slices of eggplant.

Mamma Agata's Secret
Most Eggplant Parmigiana recipes only suggest using 2 types of cheese. However, Mamma Agata uses three types of cheese to enhance the flavor of the dish, including Parmigiano, Mozzarella and smoked Provolone.

The next step is crucial: you must be very generous with all of the ingredients EXCEPT for the tomato sauce. Tomato sauce is a liquid; too much will create a soggy Eggplant Parmigiana. Build very thick eggplant layers (almost two layers in one) so that the final outcome of the Eggplant Parmigiana remains very compact once sliced into separate portions.

Now begin to layer your Eggplant Parmigiana in a baking dish as follows (8, 9, 10, 11):
1. Tomato sauce (sparingly – not too much tomato sauce)
2. Eggplant, almost two layers in one
3. Parmigiano cheese
4. Mozzarella cheese
5. Smoked Provolone or Gouda cheese
6. Fresh basil leaves

Repeat this process twice, creating three layers in total. The top/last layer of the Eggplant Parmigiana may be higher than the baking dish, this is normal (12).

NOTE: The third layer is the top layer and should contain only Mamma Agata's Tomato Sauce and Parmigiano cheese, without Mozzarella and Provolone cheese. This will help ensure that it cooks evenly in the oven without burning, making the dish nicely browned and crispy on top.

NOTE: Before placing the baking dish in the oven, place a cookie sheet or aluminium foil on the rack below your baking dish, as this dish tends to leak out (or spill over) when baking. The cookie sheet/foil will catch the drips.

Bake the Eggplant Parmigiana in a pre-heated oven for about one hour. After one hour, turn off the heat in the oven, leaving the parmigiana in the turned-off oven for an additional ten minutes with the oven door slightly open. Then, remove the Eggplant Parmigiana from the oven and let is sit at room temperature for at least forty minutes before serving. This will let it cool down and enhance the flavors. NOTE: This dish is even better the next day; simply re-heat and serve with fresh bread – delicious!

In 1960 Anita Eckberg stayed at Villa Civita, while filming la "Dolce Vita in Rome". Mamma Agata always told me that Ms. Eckberg had an amazing soft, white and milky complexion with lovely skin like a peach.
Mamma Agata remembers she would come into the kitchen and enjoy all her food but above all she loved **Mamma Agata's Eggplant Parmigiana** and the **Pappardelle with peppers and sausage.** At parties, Ms. Eckberg would eat everything on the table: pasta, pane (bread), insalata, and dolci (dessert)! She was *a real woman who truly enjoyed her food.*

I segreti della frittura
Mamma Agata's Frying Instruction

How to get the best results when frying

1. The best frying pans are ugly!!!
The frying pans we use are deep frying pans (around 3 to 4 inches deep and around 10 inches across) with a handle. You may start with a non-stick pan and then let it get ugly! You can use the same frying pan for at least 3 to 4 years. (Mamma Agata calls this her "Ugly Pan" and only uses it for deep frying.) The more seasoned the pan, the better the finished product will taste.
Once you have finished frying your food, empty the oil and use a paper towel to clean the pan. Every once in a while, gently wash the pan with water and a mild soap, especially after frying fish. Make sure that you rinse and dry your pan well after each washing.

2. Quantity of Oil
Be very generous with your oil! We recommend at least 1 litre/quart of oil. Leave one inch from the top of the oil level to the top of the pan. Do not overfill the frying pan with ingredients, as that may impact the temperature. Allow room for the ingredients to move in the pan.

3. Temperature of Oil
The oil should be very hot to achieve the best results, at least 190 degrees Celsius (374 degrees Farenheit). Before you begin frying, test the temperature of the oil by placing a small portion of the ingredients (such as a spoonful of batter) in the oil. The oil is ready when the ingredient(s) float to the top of the oil and starts to really bubble. When you are frying, the ingredients should NOT sink to the bottom and stay there. They should immediately start to float to the top and there should be a lot of bubbling. If they don't, let the oil heat more before using.

4. Quality of Oil
The quality of the oil is important. Seed oils are the best for frying because they have a high burning point. Mamma Agata uses peanut oil. Vegetable oil, especially peanut oil, doesn't burn, or impact the smell or flavor of the food.
IMPORTANT: Make sure that your guests do not have nut allergies. If you have any concerns, use a high quality vegetable oil, such as grapeseed oil.
Never use Olive Oil for frying. Olive oil is much too heavy, as it creates too strong of a flavor in the finished product, it does not hold the heat, and it burns very quickly.

5. Using Clean Oil
Be sure to use fresh oil for each batch – do not reuse the oil.

Conserva di pomodoro
Mamma Agata's Tomatoes Preserve

For centuries our family has preserved everything, including our very precious tomatoes. The traditions have been passed down through the generations, beginning with my great grandparents to my parents and into my current generation.

Our summers are rich with fresh vegetables but the winters are poor and lack the rich nutrients necessary to feed our family, so we learned to preserve our fresh fruits and vegetables from the garden so that we have enough food to carry us through the winter.

At the Hidden Treasure, we do not waste anything. For example, when the zucchini blossoms, we eat them when they are fresh. When we are lucky enough to have a bountiful harvest, we preserve the remaining fruits and vegetables such as tomatoes and eggplant to enjoy them during the cold winter months. We also harvest olives to make olive oil as well as preserve the olives themselves to eat with freshly baked bread during the long, cold winter days!

The process of making the tomatoes preserve is an important tradition in our family - not only because the tomatoes provide rich nutrients and to ensure we have tomato sauce through the winter - but the process itself of harvesting and preserving the tomatoes is a very important time that we enjoy together during the summer months – almost like our very own family tomato festival!

Each member of the family plays an important role in the preserving process: the children help to pick the tomatoes and bring them to their mothers, who wash them and hand them off to the grandparents, who process them by adding the right amount of salt and basil before boiling the tomatoes. The days preserving the tomatoes are long but we have the most amazing time together eating bread with fresh tomatoes for lunch while we sit in the garden and enjoy each other's company. This is a time that makes us all very happy!
I remember when I was a child, when I first learned to preserve the tomatoes, my sister and I always helped the family, and as a child it is truly a magical event. Today we do the same, and sadly, some members of our family are not with us anymore but they watch us from above. Some members of our family live in other cities, but our immediate family always gets together, including Papà Salvatore, Mamma Agata, Gennaro, Mario, Paola, and me.

Mamma Agata's tomatoes preserve

Here is an example of our days during the tomato harvest season:
Papà Salvatore, Mamma Agata and Gennaro wake up at 5 am and walk down to the garden to begin picking and sorting the tomatoes. They separate them according to size – for example, if they are too large or too small we cannot use them to make the preserves. A few hours later, the children and I go down to the garden to assist with the processing of the tomatoes. Mario and Paola also pick basil with my father's help and we all work closely together, laugh and joke around together – it is such a joy for everyone!
The next step in the process is for Gennaro to do, as he is the strongest member of our family and this is not an easy task! Gennaro prepares firewood and huge steel barrels that we use to boil the jarred tomatoes. The children begin to separate the basil leaves from the stems, before washing and drying the leaves and adding them to each jar. In August, the weather is very hot but we are so happy just being together and doing something good for our health and for our big family (and for our wonderful students and everyone that come to eat to Mamma Agata's).

Now, I will leave you with the thought of starting this tradition in your own home with your family, as I explain the process of preserving the tomatoes. I would love for you to begin to slowly preserve your own tomatoes so that you can gather your family together for an annual preserving festival like ours!

Here are the steps necessary to preserve tomatoes from your garden:
• First, you must seek out the right tomatoes - either Roma or Plum tomatoes;
• Wash the tomatoes and place them in basket to dry;
• Wash and dry the jars thoroughly (water in the jars is not good);
• Fill a large boiler (pot) with water and salt and bring it to boil;
• Add the tomatoes in the boiler (pot), initially the tomatoes will sink, but when they begin to float, remove them from the boiling salted water;
• Process the tomatoes with a machine that separates the seed and skin from the purée. You should be able to find this at good kitchen stores or Italian supply stores;
• Add salt to the tomato sauce. You will learn how much works best for you but we estimate 1 teaspoon per liter of tomatoes;
• In the dry glass jars, add the clean basil leaves and pour the tomato puree into the jars and close the lids tightly;
• Place the jars in the steel barrels/cauldron (the size of the steel pan can be adjusted to suit your personal needs) and cover the jars in cold water;
• Bring the water to a boil for forty-five minutes;
• After boiling for forty-five minutes, turn off the heat and leave them in the water overnight to cool down;
• The following day, remove the water from barrels and store the tomato preserves in a cool place where it can last for several years.

I hope you will have a lot of fun in this process like we do; although we are very tired after this long, hot process, we still we love it and would never change a thing!

Salsa di Pomodoro
Mamma Agata's Tomato Sauce

1 litre or 1 quart of vine-ripened roma tomatoes (puréed)
10 fresh cherry tomatoes
5 Tablespoons extra virgin olive oil
2 cloves of fresh garlic
3 fresh basil leaves

Mamma Agata's Secret
The Roma tomatoes used to make this sauce should to be vine-ripened so they are sweet. Sweet tomatoes are the key ingredient in many Italian dishes. If the tomatoes are not ripe and sweet, we recommend adding a spoonful of sugar to sweeten the sauce.

Add the olive oil, garlic and basil to a large saucepan (1). NOTE: When you add the olive oil, garlic and basil to the pan, do so all at the same time. Do not heat the oil first, then add the garlic and basil to the pan, but rather place all three ingredients into the pan at room temperature and then heat the pan.

Heat the ingredients over a high flame to release the natural oils contained in the fresh garlic, greatly enhancing the flavors of the tomato sauce. Be careful not to allow the garlic to burn or the oil to smoke. If this happens, you must throw it out and start over. The garlic and oil should only be on the high flame for one to two minutes before proceeding to the next step.

When the temperature of the oil begins to rise, add the tomato purée and fresh vine-ripened cherry tomatoes to the pan (2).
Be careful not to burn yourself or let the oil or tomatoes splash on you. You should hear a nice sizzling sound and soon you'll enjoy a wonderful aroma from the fragrant ingredients releasing their oils and combining to make this

delicious homemade tomato sauce!

Cook the sauce, first over on a high flame just until the sauce begins to boil. Then, lower the flame to simmer the sauce for a total of thirty minutes (including the time it took to bring it to a boil).

Mamma Agata's Secret
As soon as you add the Roma tomato puree to the pan, add the 10 vine-ripened cherry tomatoes (3) to the pan as well to further enhance the flavor of your sauce. This is an important step and you will be amazed how wonderful the sauce tastes in the end!

This sauce can be used for all your tomato-based recipes such as Eggplant Parmigiana or whenever you see "**Mamma Agata's Tomato Sauce**" mentioned in this book.

NOTE: Mamma Agata produces 1,200 bottles of tomato sauce every year in August using the delicious Roma tomatoes grown in our garden. We also can numerous jars of vine-ripened cherry tomatoes to use throughout the year.

Salsa con pomodorini 'freschi'
Mamma Agata's Fresh Cherry Tomato Sauce

500 gr or about 1 lb of cherry or roma tomatoes (can also be ½ of each)
3 Tablespoons extra virgin olive oil
2 cloves of fresh garlic (sliced)
2 Tablespoons fresh basil
2 pinches of sea salt
2 pinches of dried oregano

Mamma Agata's Secret
The Roma tomatoes used to make this sauce should to be vine-ripened so they are sweet. Sweet tomatoes are the key ingredient in many Italian dishes. However, if the tomatoes are not ripe and sweet, it is okay to add a spoonful of sugar to sweeten the tomato sauce.

NOTE: If you do not have access to ripe cherry tomatoes, you may use a combination of cherry and Roma tomatoes. The most important thing to keep in mind is that the tomatoes must be sweet for this sauce.

Thinly slice the garlic. Add the olive oil and garlic to a large saucepan (1) at the same time. NOTE: Do not heat the oil first, then add the garlic to the pan, but rather place the ingredients into the pan at room temperature and then heat the pan.

Chop the cherry tomatoes in half (or quarters if they are large or you are using Roma tomatoes). Add the chopped tomatoes, salt and fresh basil to the pan with the oil and garlic (2).
Cover the pan and cook over medium heat for five minutes. Add the oregano (3).
Cook your favorite pasta al dente, drain the pasta and add it to the sauce. You have to marry the ingredients before serving. Serve this dish hot with a drizzle of extra virgin olive oil.

Mamma Agata's Secret
This sauce can be used to garnish Pizza (see page 158) or Fried Pizza (see page 161).

Gnocchi di Mamma Agata

Mamma Agata's Potato Dumplings – The dough

Serves 4
1 kg or about 2 lbs potatoes
300 gr or 10 ½ oz flour ("00" or white pastry)
50 gr or 1 ¾ oz Parmigiano cheese (grated)
1 egg
4 Tablespoons extra virgin olive oil
Sea salt
Extra flour for the plate and work surface: 100 gr or 3 ½ oz flour ("00" or white pastry)

Mamma Agata's Secrets
It's best to use older potatoes for this recipe, as they contain less water and will produce a nice soft texture after they are mashed.

Add whole, unpeeled potatoes to room-temperature salted water. NOTE: Do NOT peel the potatoes or cut them because this will enhance their natural flavor.

Bring the water to a boil, reduce the heat to a low boil and cook the potatoes for 50 minutes.

Drain the potatoes and remove the skins. Mash the peeled potatoes using a potato masher or ricer and place them on top of your work station (1).

Add the grated Parmigiano cheese, the egg and flour to the potatoes and mix well forming a dough (2, 3).

Take about 1/6 of the dough and roll it into a long thin cylindrical shape (4), about one-inch wide.

Cut off small pieces of dough (about one inch long each) to create the individual dumplings/gnocchi (5).

Using your thumb, roll the dumplings across a gnocchi board (6). If you do not own a gnocchi board, you can use a fork to mark notches in your gnocchi.

Mamma Agata's Secrets
The indentations created by the gnocchi board (or fork) catch the flavors of the sauce, so please do not forget this step!

Sprinkle a little flour onto a plate (to prevent sticking) and place the gnocchi on the plate of flour (6) until you are ready to boil them.

Boil a large pan of water with salt and extra virgin olive oil (7).

Mamma Agata's Secrets
Add a dash of extra virgin olive oil and a pinch of salt to the water used to boil the dumplings to avoid the gnocchi sticking to each other.

Place the dumplings into the boiling water. The dumplings will immediately sink to the bottom of the pan, but they will slowly begin to float to the top. As soon as they are floating, remove them from the water, place them in a colander, and rinse them with cold water (to stop the cooking process).

Place the dumplings on a serving dish and drizzle extra virgin olive oil over them to prevent the dumplings from sticking to each other. Serve hot with your favorite sauce!

Gnocchi alla sorrentina
Gnocchi with tomatoes and mozzarella (called Sorrentina)

Serves 4
Mamma Agata's Gnocchi - Potato Dumplings
500 ml or 2 cups of **Mamma Agata's Tomato Sauce**
200 gr or 7 oz mozzarella cheese
10 fresh basil leaves
1-2 Tablespoons extra virgin olive oil

Prepare Mamma **Agata's Gnocchi - Potato Dumplings** (see page 63).

Prepare **Mamma Agata's Tomato Sauce** (see page 55).

In a large saucepan, add one cup of **Mamma Agata's Tomato Sauce** (1). Then add the gnocchi (2) and cover them with the remaining cup of **Mamma Agata's Tomato Sauce**.

Add the mozzarella cheese and sprinkle the Parmigianino cheese on the gnocchi (3). Cook over low heat until the cheese melts.

Mamma Agata's secret
If you wish, you may also add smoked provolone to the gnocchi (in addition to the mozzarella and Parmigiano cheeses) when you serve the gnocchi on the table.

Place the gnocchi on a serving platter and garnish with fresh basil and a little extra virgin olive oil (if you wish).

Serve hot!

Mamma Agata's Recommendation
The above recipe is for a Gnocchi Sorrentina. A delicious variation is to bake this for approximately five minutes at 180-degrees Celsius (356-degrees Fahrenheit) to marry all of the flavors beautifully.

Gnocchi con carciofi e pomodori secchi
Potato Dumplings with Sundried Tomatoes and Artichokes

Mamma Agata's Gnocchi - Potato Dumplings
10 Sun-dried tomatoes (finely minced)
4 fresh baby artichokes
1 – 2 lemons
2 cloves of garlic (finely sliced)
6 Tablespoons extra virgin olive oil
1 Tablespoon fresh parsley
2 pinches Sea salt
10 sun-dried tomatoes, for the sauce
125 ml or ½ cup water

Prepare **Mamma Agata's Gnocchi - Potato Dumplings.** Add the finely minced sun-dried tomatoes to the gnocchi dough, before rolling into cylinders (1).

Mamma Agata's Secret
You may add the minced sun-dried tomatoes to half of the gnocchi and leave the other half of the gnocchi dough plain.

The Sauce

Wash and clean the artichokes, removing the outer leaves to expose the artichoke heart (2). Cut each artichoke heart into quarters (four pieces).

IMPORTANT: If you are not able to find baby artichokes, you may use regular artichokes. Look for small, firm artichokes. For these larger artichokes, in addition to the instructions above, remove all of the stringy fibers and purple leaves in the center of the artichokes. Cut the artichoke heart into bite-sized sections, such as 6-8 pieces.

Add one to two sliced lemons (2) to a bowl of water, large enough to cover all of the artichoke pieces. Soak the artichoke pieces in the lemon water for 10 minutes to maintain their color. NOTE: If you do not soak them in lemon water, they will discolor very quickly.

Mamma Agata's Secret
Let the artichoke sit in citrus water for a minimum of 10 minutes to remove bitterness from the taste of the artichoke.

In a non-stick pan, add extra virgin olive oil, finely sliced garlic and cook over medium heat until golden brown (3).

Add the artichokes (4), fresh parsley (5) and salt. Cover the pan and sauté for ten minutes.

Add the sun-dried tomatoes (6). Cover and cook for three additional minutes.

Add a glass of water. Cover and cook for five additional minutes.

Add the gnocchi to the sauce and stir. Cook over a low flame for three additional minutes.

Serve hot!

Pappardelle con peperoni e salsiccia
Sausage and Red Pepper Pasta

Serves 4
250 gr or ½ lb long, broad pasta, wider than Fettuccini (Pappardelle pasta is best for this dish)
1 kg or 2 ¼ lbs of red and yellow sweet bell peppers
50 gr or 3 ½ Tablespoons butter – (A little less than a 1/2 stick)
4 Tablespoons extra virgin olive oil
1/2 small red or white onion (chopped)
500 gr or 1 lb sweet Italian sausage
1 kg fresh cherry tomatoes (quartered)
5 fresh basil leaves (torn)
2 pinches Sea salt
1 cup **Mamma Agata's Tomato sauce**
Peanut oil

Prepare **Mamma Agata's Tomato Sauce** (see page 55).
Wash the peppers and remove the stems. Cut each pepper in half and remove and discard the seeds from inside the peppers. Slice the peppers lengthwise, but not too thin and not to thick (1).

Sauté the peppers in peanut oil for ten to fifteen minutes until soft (2). This makes them easier to digest and also brings out the flavor.

Once the peppers are cooked, place them on a paper towel or napkin to soak up the excess oil.

In a separate pan, melt the butter and olive oil over low heat (3).

Mamma Agata's Secret
In the south of Italy, people usually use olive oil for cooking and use butter (unsalted) mainly for baking cakes and desserts. Occasionally, they use olive oil and butter together because when you cook certain dishes (such as Bolognese, Neapolitan Ragu, and this sauce) for a longer length of time, butter maintains the flavour intensity through the end of the cooking process. Olive Oil loses its flavor after 30 minutes of cooking.

Add the chopped onion (3) and cook until golden brown (but not burned).

Add the sausage to the pan and sear on all sides (4). Cover the pan and cook for an additional two minutes.

Mamma Agata's Secret
Always use sweet pork sausage rather than "spicy" or "hot" sausage. Mamma Agata's sausage is typically flavored with fennel, white wine and a pinch of pepper.

Uncover the pan and pierce the sausage with a fork on both sides, to allow the juice of the sausage to flow in the pan and enhance the flavor of the pasta sauce.
Add the peppers to the pan with the sausage (5), placing the sausage on top of the peppers. Add the chopped cherry tomatoes (6), fresh torn basil (7), salt, and the cup of **Mamma Agata's Tomato Sauce** (8) to the pan. NOTE: You can use half Roma or San Marzano and half cherry tomatoes.
Cover the pan and cook on a low flame for thirty minutes.
Once cooked, remove the sausage and cut into small pieces, and place it back into the pan.

Mamma Agata's Secret
Chop the sausage at the end of the cooking process, rather than at the beginning; this preserves the intense flavor of the sausage meat. As an alternate, you can also mince a small portion of the sausage and add it to the tomato sauce and keep the larger pieces in tact to serve on top of the pasta.

Cook the pasta in salted water until al dente. Drain the pasta and add it to the sausage and pepper sauce and cook on low heat for two additional minutes to marry the flavors.
Add a handful of grated Parmigiano cheese and serve hot!

Mamma Agata's Tips
This is a very flexible recipe because you can actually use it as two recipes in one. For example, you can prepare half of the sausage and peppers for a pasta dish, and the other half of the sausage and peppers can be served as a separate meat course.
You can keep this sauce in the refrigerator for few days. It will make a nice risotto, garnish a pizza or make a panino. It is a great thing to make when you have a hectic week and not much time to cook!

Pasta con pomodoro e ricotta
Pasta with Tomato and Ricotta Cheese

Serves 4
1 litre/quart **Mamma Agata's Tomato Sauce**
400 gr or 14 oz Spaghetti Noodles (or any pasta you prefer)
500 gr or 2 cups Ricotta Cheese
5 fresh basil leaves

Prepare **Mamma Agata's Tomato Sauce** (see page 55) and set aside.

Cook the *pasta al dente* and drain.

While the pasta is cooking, if needed, heat Mamma **Agata's Tomato Sauce** in a large skillet (1).

Add the drained pasta to the tomato sauce and stir well (2).

Place a serving of the pasta onto a plate and top with a dab of fresh ricotta cheese and a little basil.

If you prefer, add the pasta and ricotta into the pan with the sauce, stir and serve immediately with a little basil (3).

Mamma Agata Recommendation
If you wish, you may add smoked provolone cheese and/or Parmigiano cheese!

Pasta con broccoli e formaggio affumicato
BROCCOLI AND SMOKED CHEESE PASTA

Serves 4
300 gr or 10 ½ oz short pasta (Orecchiette works best with this dish)
1 kg or 1 head fresh broccoli (cut into separate florets)
1 clove garlic
2 anchovy fillets
10 cherry tomatoes (quartered)
1 Tablespoon fresh parsley
4 Tablespoon extra virgin olive oil
50 gr or 1 ¾ oz smoked Provolone or Gouda Cheese (cubed)
50 gr or 1 ¾ oz Parmigiano cheese (grated)

Clean and wash the broccoli florets and discard the main stem (1).

Boil the broccoli in salted water for five minutes. Remove and drain the broccoli, saving the water to cook the pasta. Set the broccoli aside.

Mamma Agata's Secret
Mamma Agata uses the broccoli water to cook the pasta noodles. This infuses flavor into the pasta and may add additional essential vitamins.

The Sauce
Add the extra virgin olive oil and garlic to a non-stick pan (2) and cook until lightly browned. Do not let the garlic burn, or it will become bitter. NOTE: As with all dishes, add the ingredients to the room-temperature extra virgin olive oil and cook together.

Add the anchovy fillets and cook lightly until they are dissolved.

Add the quartered cherry tomatoes and fresh parsley (3). Cover and cook the combined ingredients over medium heat for five minutes.

Add the broccoli to the pan (4) and cook for an additional five minutes (5).

Cook the pasta in the salted broccoli water until it is *al dente* (6). Drain the pasta and add it to the pan with the sauce (7).

Add the cubes of smoked Provolone (or Gouda) to the pan and cook for two additional minutes.

Place the pasta on a serving platter and garnish with a sprinkle of Parmigiano cheese.

Serve hot!

Mamma Agata with her precious grandchildren, Paola and Mario.

Pasta con zucchine tradizionale
PENNE PASTA WITH ZUCCHINI - TRADITIONAL RECIPE

Serves 4
400 gr or 14 oz short Pasta (such as penne)
1 kg or 2 – 2 ¼ lb zucchini (sliced into ¼ inch discs)
100 gr smoked Provolone or Gouda cheese (chopped into small cubes)
50 gr Parmigiano cheese (grated)
4 Tablespoons extra virgin olive oil
2 cloves garlic (finely sliced)
4 fresh basil leaves (torn)
Sea salt

Wash the zucchini. Remove and discard the tops and bottoms (1). Slice the zucchini into discs about ¼ inch thick.

Place the sliced zucchini into a bowl (or a colander if you prefer), sprinkle them with a little sea salt and let them sit for five or ten minutes, to drain some of the water from the zucchini (2).

Thinly slice the garlic. Add the olive oil and garlic to a large saucepan (3) at the same time. NOTE: Do not heat the oil first, then add the garlic to the pan, but rather place the ingredients into the pan at room temperature and then heat the pan. Cook over a low flame in a large non-stick skillet until golden brown. Add the zucchini, a pinch of salt, and the torn basil leaves to the oil and stir (4).

Mamma Agata Secret
Mamma Agata always covers the pan and cooks the combined ingredients for five minutes to enhance the many different flavors in the pan.

Cook the pasta in salted water until it is *al dente* and drain. NOTE: A pasta noodle that is short in length, such as penne, is ideal for this dish.
Add the pasta to the pan of zucchini. Stir the ingredients well (5) and continue to cook over a low flame for a few additional minutes.

Mamma Agata Secret
Mamma Agata adds Smoked Provolone or Gouda Cheese (5) to the pan of zucchini at the very end of the cooking process - just before serving to her guests.

Remove from heat, plate and serve with Parmigiano cheese. Serve hot!

Pasta con zucchine e panna
Pasta with Zucchini and Crème Fraîche

Serves 4
400 gr or 14 oz short Pasta (such as penne)
1 kg or 2 – 2 ¼ lb zucchini (sliced into ¼ inch discs)
1 small onion (finely chopped)
4 fresh basil leaves (torn)
50 gr or 3 ½ Tablespoons butter – (A little less than a 1/2 stick)
2 teaspoons sea salt
250 gr or 1 cup crème fraîche (or substitute with sour cream or buttermilk)

Wash the zucchini. Remove and discard the tops and bottoms. Slice the zucchini into discs about ¼ inch thick (1). Place the sliced zucchini into a bowl (or a colander if you prefer), sprinkle them with a little sea salt and let them sit for five or ten minutes, to drain some of the water from the zucchini (2).

In a non-stick skillet, heat the butter and the onion over a medium flame and cook until the onion is golden brown (3). Then add the zucchini, a pinch of salt and the basil leaves (4). NOTE: Use any type of onion you like, such as white, red, or sweet. Cover and cook over low heat for five additional minutes.

Cook the pasta in salted water until it is *al dente* and drain. NOTE: A pasta noodle that is short in length, such as penne, is ideal for this dish.

Add the cooked pasta to the pan with the zucchini.
Pour the crème fraîche (or sour cream/buttermilk) over the pasta and zucchini (5), and stir well over a low flame for a few minutes to warm the crème fraîche.

Mamma Agata Secret
Mamma Agata adds Smoked Provolone or Gouda Cheese to the pan of zucchini at the very end of the cooking process - just before serving to her guests.

Remove from heat, plate and serve with Parmigiano cheese. Serve hot!

Dear Brigitte,

THANK YOU FOR SHARING OUR SPECIAL DAY !

WITH LOVE AND GRATITUDE,
ELENA & MICHAEL

Pasta con gamberi e zucchine
Pasta with Shrimp and Zucchini

Serves 4
400 gr or 14 oz long or short pasta (Linguine or Paccheri is best for this dish)
1 kg or 2 pounds Shrimp or Prawns
3 whole zucchini
50 gr or 3.5 Tablespoons flour (Fine "00" or white pastry)
1 litre or 1 quart peanut or vegetable oil for frying (NOTE: Do not use olive oil)
4 Tablespoons extra virgin olive oil
2 cloves garlic (thinly sliced)
2 Tablespoons cognac
40 arugula leaves
1 pinch pepper
2 pinches of sea salt

Wash and clean the shrimp, leaving them in cold clean water for 10 minutes to drain the salt.
Wash and clean the zucchini. Remove the tops and bottoms and slice the zucchini into ¼ thick strips (1).
Place the zucchini into a colander. Sprinkle with a little salt and let them sit for five minutes, to drain some of the water from the zucchini.

Roll the zucchini in the flour until each slice is completely covered (1). Fry the zucchini until golden brown, following **Mamma Agata's Frying Instruction** (see page 47).

In a non-stick pan, add the room-temperature extra virgin olive oil and garlic (2). Cook on a low heat until the garlic is golden brown, to allow the flavors to infuse.

Add the shrimp (3), cognac (4) and a pinch of salt. Cover the pan let it cook for three minutes, just until the shrimp are opaque.

Cook the pasta in salted water until al dente. Drain the pasta. Over a low flame, add the cooked pasta to the shrimp and cook for two additional minutes.
Add the fried zucchini and garnish with the arugula leaves and a pinch of pepper.
Serve hot!

Spaghetti del contadino
Farmer's Spaghetti

Serves 4
400 gr or 14 oz pasta (Spaghetti works best with this dish)
1 kg or 1 ¼ lb ripe cherry tomatoes -- the riper the better!
1 Tablespoon fresh parsley (finely chopped)
6 Tablespoons extra virgin olive oil
4 cloves garlic (finely sliced)
1 teaspoon dried oregano
2 dozen (i.e. 24) green olives (with or without pits)
2 dozen (i.e. 24) black olives (with or without pits)
1 Tablespoon capers (packed in salt, if available, and rinsed)
1 cup fresh arugula leaves

Cut the cherry tomatoes in half and place them in a bowl (1) with the chopped parsley (2). NOTE: If the cherry tomatoes are very large, you'll need to cut them into quarters.

Mamma Agata's Secret
The riper the cherry tomatoes, the sweeter and more delicious they are in this recipe!

Add the parsley to the tomatoes before cooking them in oil to enhance the flavor of the tomatoes. As the parsley sautés in the hot oil, it will lose some of its flavor. NOTE: If the parsley burns, it becomes toxic.

Thinly slice the garlic (3) and add it to the room-temperature extra virgin olive oil. Slowly heat the garlic and oil over a very low temperature so that the flavor of the garlic will infuse the oil as it cooking.

Mamma Agata's Secret
Add the garlic to room temperature oil and gently heat them both at the same time because if you heat the olive oil before you add the garlic, the oil will be too hot and it will burn the garlic, making it bitter.

When the oil and garlic are warm and have been gently cooked, add the halved cherry tomatoes, parsley (4), oregano, green olives (5), black olives (6) and rinsed capers (7) to the pan.

Mamma Agata's Secret
Mamma Agata uses capers preserved in salt, as they are more flavorful. If you can find them, be sure to rinse them in water before using to avoid a sauce that is too salty. Since they still retain some of their salt even after washing, they will properly season this dish. If you use capers preserved in brine, you may need to add salt in order to balance the flavors.

Boil the pasta until it is al dente. Drain the spaghetti and add to the pan with the sauce (8). Cook for an additional two minutes.

Add the arugula leaves (8) to the pasta and sauce just prior to serving so that it does not lose its flavor in the cooking process.

Serve hot with a drizzle of olive oil to further enhance the flavors in the dish and enjoy!

In 1962, Jacqueline Kennedy visited the Amalfi Coast with her son "John John" and stayed at the storied Villa Civita where Mamma Agata worked as a cook. Mamma Agata always told me that Jacqueline was such an elegant and simple woman. She loved **Mamma Agata's Spaghetti of the Farmer**, and she loved Mamma's simple and genuine food.
Often, Jacqueline Kennedy joined her in the kitchen for a cup of coffee and, after drinking it, she would wash the cup and place it back in the cupboard. Mamma Agata would always say to me "Jacqueline Kennedy was *a real lady*"!

Base per Risotto
Basic preparation for Risotto

Serves 4
6 Tablespoons extra virgin olive oil
1 Tablespoon butter
300 gr or 1 1/3 cup Carnaroli rice
1 small onion (thinly sliced)
125 ml or ½ cup white wine
1 litre or 1 quart broth, such as vegetable, chicken, beef, fish
(depending on your final ingredients)

Heat the olive oil and butter in a large pan over low heat (1).
Add the onions and cook until golden brown (2).
Once the onions are golden brown, add the rice to the pan (3) and stir the rice until it becomes translucent (4); this will allow the risotto to begin to absorb the flavors of the onion, butter and olive oil.

Add the wine to the risotto (5) and cook for about five minutes, until the wine is absorbed.
Add a ladle of broth (6). Cook the rice in the broth for five to eight minutes per ladle, allowing the rice to absorb the broth before adding any more.

After you add the last ladle of broth to the rice, add your favorite ingredients to the rice (some of Mamma's favorites are pumpkin, peas, sausage or mushrooms), and cook the rice, broth and vegetables until the risotto is fully cooked *al dente*.
A sprinkle of cheese such as Parmigiano is a nice finishing touch and can be added to the top of the risotto at the end. Serve immediately!

Risotto al limone
Mamma Agata's Lemon Risotto

Serves 4
300 gr or 1 1/3 cup Carnaroli rice
100 gr or 7 Tablespoons butter
Juice of 2 lemons
Zest of 1 lemon (finely grated)
1 litre or 1 quart vegetable broth
250 gr or 1 cup crème fraîche

Heat the butter in a large pan over low heat (1) and add the rice to the pan (2).

Stir the rice until it becomes translucent (3); this will allow the risotto to begin to absorb the flavors.

Add the lemon juice (4) and grated lemon zest (5) to the pan and a pinch of salt and cook until the liquid is absorbed.

Add a ladle of broth (6). Cook the rice in the broth for five to eight minutes per ladle, allowing the rice to absorb the broth before adding any more.

Once the liquid has been fully absorbed by the rice and it is fully cooked *(al dente)*, add crème fraîche to the pan over low heat. Stir well for two minutes until the cream is warm, but not boiling.

Plate the risotto and garnish with lemon zest. Also, a sprinkle of a complimenting cheese, such as Parmigiano, may be a nice touch. Serve immediately!

Risotto con funghi e salsiccia
Risotto with Mushrooms and Sausage

Serves 4

300 gr or 1 1/3 cup Carnaroli rice
1 small onion (thinly sliced)
200 gr or ¾ to 1 lb sweet Italian sausage
100 gr or 3 – 3 ½ oz dried mushrooms
6 Tablespoons extra virgin olive oil
1 Tablespoon butter
125 ml or ½ cup white wine
1 litre or 1 quart vegetable broth

Heat the olive oil and butter in a large pan over low heat.
Add the onions and cook until golden brown (1).

Once the onions are golden brown, add the rice to the pan (2) and stir the rice until it becomes translucent (3); this will allow the risotto to begin to absorb the flavors of the onion, butter and olive oil.

Add the wine to the risotto (4) and cook for about five minutes, until the wine is absorbed.
Add sausage to the risotto (5) and cook for three minutes each side to sear the sausage.
Add a ladle of broth (5) to the risotto. Cook the rice in the broth for five to eight minutes per ladle, allowing the rice to absorb the broth before adding any more.
Add the mushrooms to the risotto (6) and cook for ten more minutes, until all of the liquid has been absorbed by the rice.
Also, a sprinkle of a complimenting cheese, such as Parmigiano may be a nice touch as well as some freshly ground black pepper. Serve immediately!

SOMMELIER *Gennaro Petti*

This is the story of my dear husband Gennaro. As with all of us, Gennaro's life has not been easy but his will to live a good life was much stronger than the hardships, and he never felt the sense of defeat!

When Gennaro and I were married, he quickly became a very important part of our family, and he also continues to provide a critical piece of our culinary puzzle – as a professionally trained Sommelier. But there is much more to him than being a great husband and Sommelier, so please keep reading and you will see what I mean.

When Gennaro was a boy of only 12 years, he started to show an intense desire to learn how to cook – a rare occurrence for a school boy his age. This really pleased his mother, a very strong and dynamic woman who worked in a stone cave by day, and cared for Gennaro and his brother and his sister in the evenings. Gennaro began helping his mother prepare their evening meals, as well as the big Sunday family dinner. His mother was very lucky and grateful to have help in the kitchen from her young son, as most boys his age would prefer to play soccer or hang out in the piazza with their friends – definitely not in the kitchen with their mother!

When Gennaro turned 15, he realized he would need money in order to pursue an education in engineering, and so he took odd jobs during the summers to save enough money to pay for his tuition.

His first summer job was in a butcher shop, where he learned great meat such as how to recognize quality products, how to clean and prepare the different cuts and lastly, how to preserve and cook meat properly.
The following summer, Gennaro went to work in a tomato production factory – a job so difficult that it made his hair fall out – literally! The factory was not air conditioned and it was unbearably hot in the summer months, especially with the canning equipment running. The only good thing that came out of this experience was that he learned as much as one can learn about tomatoes – from the selection process (good tomatoes vs. bad tomatoes) to the handling process. The factory also preserved peaches and beans, so he learned a little about that too.
Then the next summer, he went to work in a food factory that produced many types of cheese, prosciutto, ham, pasta, and many more types of food and wine, sparking his interest.

Sommelier Gennaro Petti

Gennaro finally graduated from engineering school with honours, and began utilizing his engineering skills immediately; he was a very good engineer and highly sought after in his profession. In fact, he was so busy that he had to temporarily abandon his love of food and wine to focus solely on engineering.
But destiny was knocking on his door, and when we met in 1994, we immediately knew that we wanted to incorporate his passion for food and wine into our offers at the Hidden Treasure.

Thankfully for us, Gennaro eventually decided to take the necessary steps to become a professional Sommelier. After many years of intensive training, he graduated with the highest score possible on the test, and he quickly became one of the most popular Sommeliers on the Amalfi Coast. He is now a member of the Associazione Italiana Sommelier, (Italian order of the Sommelier) and his wine cellar now holds more than 100 bottles of fine wines with a special emphasis on wines from the Campania region. He continues to add new wines to his cellar whenever he has the opportunity to visit local wineries. He has visited some of the most important wineries in our region, as well as small, boutique wineries, many of which offer spectacular wines that are hard to find outside of Italy.

As Gennaro is on a never-ending quest to feed his deep passion for the culinary arts, he did not stop at becoming a professional Sommelier but he continued his food studies by taking cheese courses that include studying the production process, preservation, tasting and how to tell a great cheese from a lesser quality one and after many long hours of studying, Gennaro became a "Maestro degustatore di formaggio" otherwise known as a professional cheese taster!

In addition to being a professional Sommelier and cheese taster, Gennaro is also a truly wonderful chef – especially when it comes to preparing fresh fish and seafood – and he cooks these dishes with the same passion he has for his wine and cheese.

When you join us for either a dinner or a wine tasting, you and your guests will see firsthand that Gennaro exudes his passion through his cooking and wine pairings, including also a tasting of grappa that he has collected for years and is a big connoisseur. Speaking of grappa, we also are very proud of our delicious homemade limoncello – the famous southern Italian liqueur.

Gennaro also makes many other interesting homemade liqueurs from scratch, using tangerines, apricots and fennel. An experience with him will be memorable. And perhaps, life changing with the knowledge that he will pass on to you!

And guess what? His story does not stop there, as his quest for knowledge is nearly insatiable and he continued his culinary education by taking classes on olive oils.

Gennaro can now distinguish between various types of olive oil and production methods. The same year he became a professional cheese taster, he also earned the title of professional olive oil taster!

Of course it was natural for us to open a wine school where Gennaro teaches people to discern what a good wine is and empower them with the knowledge to face a bottle or a glass with the confidence to say – wow, I know so much more about this wine, thanks to Gennaro!

Unlike some classes, Gennaro teaches his students in a very simple way – you will learn how to analyze a wine using your natural senses of sight, smell and taste. You'll also learn all about the production process including the grape varietals and fermentation process.

Naturally, wine pairs with cheese, so we incorporate a cheese tasting to our wine classes where we offer students to savor up to 10 different varieties of cheeses that come from Campania. We explain to our guests where they are produced and how to serve them with sweet toppings such as Mamma Agata's delicious homemade chestnut honey and pear marmalade, which of course our guests get to taste!

Since olive oil is a staple in all Italian pantries, we thought it would be a nice touch to include an olive oil tasting to our wine and cheese tasting. Our goal is to teach people the most important information about the olive oil, such as what to buy, what to use and when, and how to store and protect the flavours of a good olive oil.
And of course, we must serve delicious wine with delicious food too. So, Gennaro

Sommelier Gennaro Petti

prepares for the course by cooking a few wonderful house specialties for our students to enjoy along with the wine, and at the end of the meal he serves grappa with pastries and chocolate.

If you've already read the story of Mamma Agata's life, you might see that Gennaro's life is parallel to that of Mamma's. They both share a huge passion for cooking that started from a very young age, and they both spent their years as young adults working in the culinary field and now of course, they share their passion for food and wine with the guests at the Hidden Treasure.
In fact, Gennaro cooks side-by-side with Mamma Agata each day. They are both such great cooks, each with their own different techniques but both reaching the same amazing results – delicious food, wonderful flavors and *Simple and Genuine* cooking!

Gennaro is also a wonderful student of Mamma Agata and he is slowly learning all of Mamma Agata's many cooking secrets and one day, he will be the perfect cooking instructor too.

I know in my heart that Gennaro will never stop studying and adding to his already vast culinary and wine knowledge as he has an endless energy and love for people and food and wine is a driving force that he will continue to seek and fulfill his inner cravings and express his love of teaching to anyone who has the pleasure to meet him during a visit to our Hidden Treasure in Ravello.

Arrosto di' maiale
Roasted Pork Loin

Serves 4
1 kg or about 2 – 2 ½ lbs pork loin
8 sage leaves
2 rosemary sprigs
50 gr or 3 ½ Tablespoons butter
5 Tablespoons extra virgin olive oil

250 ml or 1 cup white wine
1 medium white onion (roughly diced)
2 carrots (roughly chopped)
1 celery stalk (roughly chopped)
2 Tablespoons Sea salt
1 mt. or 1 yard of kitchen twine to wrap the pork

Wrap the outside edges of pork loin with fresh sage leaves and rosemary sprigs, using a piece of kitchen twine to hold the herbs in place (1).

Mamma Agata's Secret
Wrapping the outside edges of the pork loin with fresh sage leaves and rosemary sprigs infuses the flavors of the herbs into the pork and enhances the flavors of the meat.

In a large pan, melt the butter and extra virgin olive oil over a low flame (2).

Mamma Agata's Secret
In the south of Italy, people usually use olive oil for cooking and use butter (unsalted) mainly for baking cakes and desserts. Occasionally, they use olive oil and butter together because when you cook certain dishes (such as Bolognese, Neapolitan Ragu, and this sauce) for a longer length of time, butter maintains the flavour intensity through the end of the cooking process. Olive Oil loses its flavor after thirty minutes of cooking.

Add the pork loin to the pan and sear all sides of the meat to seal in the flavor (2). Add a portion of salt to each side of the pork loin as you brown the meat in the pan. Continue turning the meat until all sides have been browned. Use a wooden spoon to turn the pork to release its natural oils without burning it.

Mamma Agata's Secret
Mamma Agata recommends using a wooden spoon and not use a sharp object as it may pierce your non-stick surface of the pan and could ruin the pan.

Once the pork is brown on all sides, pour the white wine over the meat (3). Cover and cook over a low flame for about two minutes.

Add the carrots, celery (4), and onion (5) to the pan. Cover and cook over low heat for one hour, gently turning the pork every fifteen minutes.

Remove the pan from the heat, and let it sit for ten to fifteen minutes before serving.

Mamma Agata's Secret
The vegetables used in the cooking process may be served as a side dish, or they can be pureed and served over the top of the pork roast.

Arrosto di vitello
Veal Roast

Serves 4
1 kg or 2 – 2 ½ lbs veal or beef shoulder roast
10 fresh sage leaves
3 fresh rosemary sprigs
250 gr or 1.1 cups (2 ¼ sticks) unsalted butter
2 cloves garlic
250 ml or 1 cup white wine
A few pinches Sea salt

Wrap the outside edges of roast with sage leaves and rosemary sprigs, wrapping it with twine to hold the herbs in place (1).

Mamma Agata's Secret
Wrapping the outside edges of the roast with fresh sage leaves and rosemary sprigs infuses the flavors of the herbs into the pork and enhances the flavors of the meat.

In a pan, melt the butter and garlic together. Cook over low to medium heat (2). Do not allow the butter and garlic to burn! Once the butter is melted, add the roast to the pan (2) and sear all sides of the meat to seal in the flavour. Add the salt to each side of the roast as you brown it in the pan for a total of about five minutes altogether. Use a wooden spoon to turn the roast to release its natural oils without burning it.

Mamma Agata's Secret
Mamma Agata recommends using a wooden spoon and not use a sharp object as it may pierce your non-stick surface of the pan and could ruin the pan.

Add white wine to the roast (3), cover the pan and simmer for another twenty minutes.
At this point, the roast should be medium rare, with a lovely pink color inside. You may plate, slice and serve the roast immediately!

NOTE: If you prefer the meat well done, slice the roast and place it back into the pan in its own juice and cook to your desired temperature.

Coniglio con pomodoro e olive
Mamma Agata's Rabbit with Tomato and Olives

Serves 4
1 kg or 2 – 2 ½ lb rabbit (cut into pieces)
A few pinches Sea salt
3 Tablespoons white vinegar
4 Tablespoons extra virgin olive oil
½ white onion (chopped)
2 bay leaves
10 cherry tomatoes (halved)
20 black olives (pitted)
20 green olives (pitted)

Clean and wash the rabbit, and cut into small pieces with the bone on (1). Heat a non-stick pan on the stovetop over a high flame/heat until it becomes very hot (1).

Mamma Agata's Secret
Do not add oil to the pan, as this will help sear in the juices of the rabbit once it is placed on the heat.

Add the rabbit to the pan and brown the meat on both sides, adding a pinch of salt to each side (1).
Add white vinegar to the pan. Cover and cook over medium heat for two minutes, until the juices in the pan evaporate.

Mamma Agata's Secret
The vinegar helps to reduce some of the gamey flavor of rabbit.

Reduce the heat. Add the chopped onions (2), olive oil (3) and bay leaves to the pan. Cover and cook for an additional five minutes. Add the cherry tomatoes (4) and olives (5, 6) to the pan. Cover and cook for an additional fifteen minutes.
Remove from the heat and serve hot!

Coniglio Fritto
Fried Rabbit

Serves 4
1 kg or 2 – 2 ½ lbs rabbit
10 cloves garlic
2 fresh rosemary sprigs
5 fresh sage leaves
1 litre or 1 quart peanut or vegetable oil for frying (NOTE: Do not use olive oil)

Clean and wash the rabbit, and cut into small pieces with the bone on.

Follow **Mamma Agata's Frying Instructions** (see page 47).

Add the garlic cloves, sage and rosemary to the cold frying oil before heating (1). Heat the oil to the proper frying temperature.

Mamma Agata's Secret
Adding the garlic and herbs to the frying oil will flavor the oil immensely, and further reduce the gamey flavor of the rabbit.

Add the rabbit and fry it for a few minutes (2), until it turns golden brown.

Remove from the oil and drain (on paper towels). Serve hot!

Mamma Agata's Secret
As with all fried foods, this should be eaten immediately for best results! Enjoy!

Pollo al limone
Mamma Agata's famous Lemon Chicken

Serves 4
½ whole chicken (cut into pieces with the skins on)
5 cloves garlic (chopped in half)
2 teaspoons sea salt
1 Tablespoon dried sage
1 Tablespoon dried rosemary
250 ml or 1 cup cooking wine (or Mamma Agata's Wine Infusion – see below)
1 Tablespoon Italian flat-leaf parsley (coarsely chopped)
Juice of 2 large lemons (4 lemons, if small)

Mamma Agata Wine Infusion:
Prepare this at least four days BEFORE making this dish:
1 bottle white wine
2 fresh rosemary sprigs
8 fresh sage leaves
Place the rosemary sprigs and the sage leaves in a warm oven for few minutes until you begin to smell the scent of the herbs. Then, immediately remove them from the oven and place them in the bottle with the white wine. Close the bottle and set it aside for at least four days to infuse with the wine before preparing this recipe.

Clean the chicken and separate into pieces with the bone and skin on (1). Do not remove the skins.

Mamma Agata's Secrets
Use a non-stick pan to make this recipe. A non-stick pan allows the chicken to seal in the flavor without burning the skin or sticking to the pan when it is seared over a high flame. Having the chicken a little crowded in the pan is suggested, as the juices released from the pieces are more concentrated.

Add the garlic to a dry non-stick pan (1).

Mamma Agata's Secret
Do not add oil to the pan, as this will help sear in the juices of the chicken once it is placed on the heat.

Heat the garlic over a high flame until the garlic becomes very hot, but not burned (1). Use a wooden spoon to turn the garlic to release its natural oils without burning it.

Mamma Agata's Secret
Mamma Agata recommends using a wooden spoon and not use a sharp object as it may pierce your non-stick surface of the pan and could ruin the pan.

Add the chicken to the pan, one piece at a time, skin side down (1). You should hear the chicken sizzle. This is an important step as you must sear in the flavor to seal the juices in the chicken. Add half of the sea salt, rosemary and sage to the top of the chicken (2, 3). Once the skin of the chicken has caramelized (i.e. is golden brown), turn the chicken over. Add the remaining salt, rosemary and sage to the other side of the chicken to caramelize this side too.

Mamma Agata's Secrets
At this point, we are just searing in the flavors and not actually cooking the chicken yet.

After both sides are caramelized, lower the flame, cover the pan and cook over low heat for about twenty minutes (4).

Mamma Agata's Secrets
Do not uncover the lid while it is cooking or else it will break the moisture barrier and may become dry. The lid helps to maintain the moisture in the chicken while it is cooking. If you use a clear lid, you'll see the steam on the lid turn back into liquid and fall back down into the pan (4).

After twenty minutes, you should see the natural juices of the chicken have reduced. Now, you may uncover the chicken and add the wine to the pan (5). Continue cooking over low heat until the wine reduces.

Mamma Agata's Secrets
Infuse the wine with fresh rosemary and sage leaves for four days (recipe included above) prior to preparing this dish, as this will enhance the flavor of the chicken.

Add at the end (just before serving) chopped parsley (6, 7) and fresh lemon juice (8).

Serve immediately!

Mamma Agata's Secrets
Add the lemon juice and parsley to the chicken at the very end of the cooking process. If the lemon juice is added to the pan and cooked for too long, it will become bitter.

Useful tip:
This is a recipe that can be prepared a few hours in advance, before your family or friends arrive. Complete the steps of the recipe up to pouring the wine over the chicken and stir. Then, immediately cover and remove the pan from the flame/heat to stop the cooking process. Keep covered and set it aside until you are ready to serve it. When your family arrives, cook the chicken, following the directions in the recipe above from that point forward. By preparing the chicken in advance, you'll be able to enjoy your company and have a wonderful meal to present to them, without having to spend so much time in the kitchen during their visit!

Pollo alla cacciatora

HUNTER STYLE CHICKEN

Serves 4
½ of a whole chicken
100 gr or 1/8 lb bacon (cut into 2-inch strips)
2 Tablespoons extra virgin olive oil
1 onion (quartered and sliced)
1 rosemary sprig
2 sweet red bell peppers (seeded and cut into large chunks)
375 ml or 1½ cups **Mamma Agata's Tomato Sauce**
(or about 20 fresh cherry tomatoes, if in season. NOTE: They must be very ripe and sweet!)
2 pinches Sea salt
250 ml or 1 cup white wine
100 gr or 1 cup mushrooms (whole)

Optional but recommended: prepare **Mamma Agata's Tomato Sauce** (see pag. 55).

Clean the chicken and separate into pieces with the bone and skin on.

Mamma Agata's Secret
To enhance the flavor of this dish, leaving the skin on the chicken and the bones intact.

On a separate workspace from the chicken, quarter and slice the onion, and place in a bowl. Seed and cut the peppers and place in a separate bowl (1).

In a large non-stick pan, add the olive oil and bacon (2).

Cook on medium heat until the bacon is golden brown, and then add the pieces of chicken to the pan (3).

Sear the chicken on both sides.

After searing, cook the chicken over low heat and slowly add the following ingredients to the pan, one at a time:

• Rosemary sprig (4)
• Onions (5)
• Sweet red bell peppers (6)
• White wine (7)
• **Mamma Agata's Tomato Sauce** (8) or 20 fresh cherry tomatoes
• 2 pinches sea salt
Cover the pan and let the ingredients simmer for twenty minutes.

Add the mushrooms (9) to the pan and continue to cook over low heat for five additional minutes.

Remove from the heat and serve hot!

Polpette di Mamma Agata
Mamma Agata's Meatballs

200 gr or 7 oz bread (stale)
125 ml or ½ cup water
125 ml or ½ cup whole milk
½ kg or 1 lb ground meat: ½ ground beef and ½ ground pork
50 gr or 3 ½ Tablespoons (1 ¾ oz) grated Parmigiano cheese
3 eggs
1 Tablespoon chopped fresh parsley
1 garlic clove (very finely grated)
100 gr or 7 Tablespoons (3 ½ oz) flour ("00" or white pastry)
1 litre or 1 quart peanut or vegetable oil for frying (NOTE: Do not use olive oil)

Remove the crust from the bread and discard it (1).

Soak the bread in milk and water for five minutes to soften the bread, before mixing it with the ground beef and pork mixture (2).

Stir the mixture well and squeeze out the excess milk and water with your hands (3, 4).

Place the moist bread on a plate and set aside (4).

Combine the following ingredients with your hands in a large mixing bowl (5-11):
- Ground beef and pork mixture (5)
- Moist bread (6)
- Parmigiano cheese (grated) (7)
- Eggs (8)
- Parsley (chopped) (9)
- Garlic (finely grated) (10)

Mamma Agata's Secret
Only a little garlic is needed to make these meatballs perfect. If you use too much, you will only taste the garlic. Also, Mamma Agata prefers NOT to use a garlic press, but to grate or finely chop the garlic.

Place some flour on a clean plate. After combining all meatball ingredients (11), take a small amount of the mixture and roll it in between the palms of your hands (12).
Roll the meatball in the flour (13). Place it on a clean plate (14) and repeat this process until you run out of the meat mixture (Meatballs should be about the size of a golf ball – no larger).

Follow **Mamma Agata's Frying Instructions** (see page 47) to fry the meatballs until they are golden brown (15). Remove them from the oil and then drain (on a paper towel).

Serve warm!

Alternative to frying:
A healthier alternative to frying the meatballs is to place them into an oven-proof dish with a drizzle of olive oil and bake them at 150 degrees Celsius (or 325 degrees Fahrenheit) until they are golden brown.

Serving suggestions include the following:
1. As appetizers
2. Simmered in Mamma Agata's delicious Tomato Sauce
3. Sliced and added to a baked pasta dishes, such as a lasagna

Meat

Polpette al pomodoro
Meatballs in Tomato Sauce

Serves 4
200 gr or 7 oz bread (stale)
125 ml or ½ cup milk
125 ml or ½ cup water
½ kg or 1 lb ground meat: ½ ground beef and ½ ground pork
50 gr or 3 ½ Tablespoons (1 ¾ oz) Parmigiano cheese (grated)
1 garlic clove (finely grated)
1 Tablespoon parsley (chopped)
3 eggs
2 Tablespoons or ¼ cup dried currants
2 Tablespoons or ¼ cup pine nuts
100 gr or 7 Tablespoons (3 ½ oz) flour (Fine "00" or white pastry)
1 litre or 1 quart peanut or vegetable oil for frying (NOTE: Do not use olive oil)
1 litre or quart of **Mamma Agata's Tomato Sauce**

Remove the crust from the bread and discard it. Soak the bread in milk and water for five minutes to soften the bread, before mixing it with the ground beef and pork mixture. Stir the mixture well and squeeze out the excess milk and water with your hands. Place the moist bread on a plate and set aside.

Combine the following ingredients with your hands in a large mixing bowl (1):
- Ground beef and pork mixture
- Moist bread
- Parmigiano cheese (grated)
- Eggs
- Parsley (chopped)
- Garlic (finely grated)
- Dried currants
- Pine nuts

(NOTE: These ingredients and instructions are identical to **Mamma Agata's Meatballs** (see pages 129-130), plus the addition of currants and pine nuts. Feel free to look at the pictures in the **Mamma Agata's Meatballs** recipe if that provides additional guidance.

Mamma Agata's Secret
Only a little garlic is needed to make these meatballs perfect. If you use too much, you will only taste the garlic. Also, Mamma Agata prefers NOT to use a garlic press, but to grate or finely chop the garlic.

Place some flour on a clean plate. After combining all meatball ingredients, take a small amount of the mixture and roll it into oblong shapes, similar to American footballs - about 4 inches long (see picture 2). Roll the meatball in the flour. Place it on a clean plate and repeat this process until you run out of the meat mixture.

Follow **Mamma Agata's Frying Instructions** (see page 47) to fry the meatballs for a few minutes (3), drain (on a paper towel) and put them on a clean plate (4) NOTE: Frying the meatballs will sear them. You do not need to fry the meatballs for too long, as they will continue cooking further after they are fried.

Prepare **Mamma Agata's Tomato Sauce** (see page 55).
Add the meatballs to the prepared Mamma Agata's Tomato Sauce on the stovetop; cover and simmer for about fifteen minutes (5).

Serve hot with a nice Mediterranean salad!

Spezzatino di carne con patate e carote
Beef Stew with Potatoes and Carrots

Serves 4

1 kg or 2 ¼ lbs beef (chuck or similar cut of beef for stewing)
50 gr or 3 ½ Tablespoons flour
56 gr or 4 Tablespoons extra virgin olive oil
1 onion (quartered and sliced)
5 sage leaves
125 ml or ½ cup white wine
4 potatoes (cut into large chunks)
2 carrots (cut into large chunks)
2 pinches Sea salt
1 cup water

Cut the beef into cubes and dip the pieces of beef in flour to coat. Set aside.
In a pan, add the extra virgin olive oil and sliced onions (1) and cook until the onions are golden brown.

Mamma Agata's Secret
Always add ingredients to room-temperature extra virgin olive oil and cook from room temperature. This will help infuse the flavors into the oil.

Add the cubes of beef (2), a pinch of salt to the pan with the onions. Sear the beef, stirring the meat so that it browns evenly (3).
When the beef has browned, add the sage leaves and the white wine (4). Cover and simmer for an additional ten minutes.
Add a cup of water to the pan, along with the potatoes and carrots (5), and another pinch of salt. Cover and cook for an additional twenty minutes or until vegetables are tender.
Serve hot!

Mamma Agata's *Fishing Lesson*

They say that the best way to learn how to prepare fresh fish is to learn from the fishermen themselves, since they naturally possess a deep respect and love of the sea! True fisherman seem to have a gift for capturing the impossible - maintaining the intense flavors of the sea in the fish, even after the fish has been cooked. Mamma Agata inherited this special gift at the very young age of thirteen. As with everything else, she demanded simple and genuine flavours in her cooking, and of course, this included using only the very freshest fish she could possibly find.

In her quest for fresh fish, Mamma Agata met an old fisherman in Amalfi who taught her the secrets of preparing the fish. Mamma Agata immediately began incorporating them into her meal preparation. She would buy fresh produce from the local markets, and buy the fresh fish directly from the fisherman, whom she spoke with and learned how to cook the fish to bring out its best. Everyone loved the simple ways of "Baby Agata", who was wise beyond her years, with her careful and genuine approach to cooking the local fish, vegetables and herbs.

Pesce al forno del marinaio
Fisherman's Baked Fish

Serves 4
1 whole fresh fish - approximately 700 gr to 1kg (1.5 to 1.75 pounds)
125 ml or ½ cup white wine
125 ml or ½ cup water
2 Tablespoons fresh parsley (chopped)
2 cloves garlic (thinly sliced)
1 teaspoon Sea salt
Juice of 2 lemons
8 Tablespoons extra virgin olive oil

Clean and prepare the fish, i.e. remove the insides and the scales of the fish. NOTE: Your local fishmonger can help you with this.

Pre-heat the oven to 160 degrees Celsius (320 degrees Fahrenheit).
Place the fish in an ovenproof dish. Carefully open the inside of the fish and sprinkle it with a pinch of sea salt (1). Carefully stuff the inside of the fish with the half of the garlic (2) and half of the chopped parsley (3). Close the fish.

Drizzle the top of the fish with olive oil and another pinch of sea salt (4). Turn the fish over and repeat this process (4) so both sides are oiled and salted.

Pour the white wine and water over the fish. Add the remainder of the garlic and fresh parsley to the top of the fish.
Place the fish in the pre-heated oven for approximately fifteen minutes.

Remove parsley and garlic from the fish. Debone and filet. Place the filets back into the pan and squeeze the fresh lemon juice over the filet. Place the lemon filets back in the oven to warm them up for two more minutes.

Place the fish on a large serving platter and top with the wine and lemon juice from the bottom of the baking dish.

Serve hot!

Pesce al gratin
Baked Fish with Italian Breadcrumbs

Serves 4
4 fish fillets (cod or another similar mild, white flaky fish)
1 Tablespoon fresh parsley (finely chopped)
1 teaspoon fresh garlic (finely chopped)
4 Tablespoons breadcrumbs
2 Tablespoons Parmigiano cheese (grated)
2 pinches Sea salt
6 Tablespoons extra virgin olive oil
Fresh parsley to garnish

Clean, debone, and fillet the fish (if not already that way from the fishmonger). NOTE: You may use filets with or without the skin. Pre-heat the oven to 160 degrees Celsius or 325 degrees Fahrenheit.

On a separate workspace, finely chop the parsley (1) and garlic. Place them in a bowl with the breadcrumbs, Parmigiano cheese and salt. Mix well (2).
Place half of the breadcrumb mixture into an ovenproof dish (3). Drizzle two tablespoons of olive oil over the breadcrumb mixture and place the fish on top. NOTE: If the fish has the skin on, place the fish in the ovenproof dish with the skin facing up (3).

Drizzle olive oil over the fish (4) and then add the remainder of the breadcrumb mixture to the top of the fish (5).
Place the fish in the pre-heated oven and cook for ten minutes. Plate and serve the fish with a garnish of parsley. Serve hot!

Totani e patate
SQUID WITH POTATOES

Serves 4
1 kg or 2–2 ½ lbs squid (Totani)
2 baking potatoes
2 cloves garlic (finely sliced)
6 Tablespoons extra virgin olive oil
2 Tablespoons fresh parsley (chopped)
10 cherry tomatoes
1 teaspoon dried oregano
½ cup white wine
1 teaspoon Sea salt
1 cup water

Wash and clean the squid. Chop the squid into small pieces, including the tentacles and place it into a mixing bowl (1).
Peel and cut the potatoes into cubes and cover them with water in a separate to avoid any discolouring. Set aside.
In a saucepan, add room-temperature extra virgin olive oil, finely sliced garlic and parsley (2). Heat over a low flame for about two minutes until the garlic is golden brown. NOTE: Be careful not to burn the parsley, as it becomes toxic when overcooked.

Mamma Agata's Secret
Always add ingredients to room-temperature extra virgin olive oil and cook from room temperature. This will help infuse the flavors into the oil.

Add the squid (3) and the oregano (4) to the pan.
Add the wine (5), cover the pan and cook for five minutes.
Add the cherry tomatoes, potatoes, salt and a cup of water to the pan (6). Cover the pan and simmer over a low heat until the potatoes are fully cooked (about fifteen minutes).

Remove the ingredients from the heat and serve!

Totani 'imbottiti'
STUFFED SQUID

Serves 4
4 large squid (Totani)
50 gr or ¼ cup bread crumbs
50 gr or ¼ cup Parmigiano cheese (grated)
1 Tablespoon capers
10 whole black olives (pitted and chopped)
1 bunch fresh parsley (finely chopped)
750 ml or 3 cups tomato purée
5 Tablespoons extra virgin olive oil
2 cloves garlic (finely chopped)
A pinch dried oregano, to garnish
Toothpicks

Wash and clean the squid. On a chopping board, separate the squid's body from the tentacles and chop the tentacles into small pieces (1). On a separate workspace, chop the fresh parsley. Add the capers, black olives, and about half of the parsley to the chopped tentacles and stir to create the tentacle mixture (2).

Drizzle the bottom of a skillet with a small amount of extra virgin olive oil. Before heating the oil, add the tentacle mixture to the pan (capers, olives, parsley, tentacles). Sauté for five minutes over medium to low heat (3).

Mamma Agata's Secret
Always add ingredients to room temperature extra virgin olive oil and cook from room temperature. This will help infuse the flavors into the oil.

Add the bread crumbs and Parmigiano cheese (4) to the pan. Mix well for one minute and remove the pan from the heat (5).

Stuff the squids with the ingredients from the pan (6). Insert a toothpick or two through the squid to close the top and keep the ingredients from falling out - one or two toothpicks should be all that is necessary (7, 8). In a clean saucepan, add extra virgin olive oil and garlic. Sauté until the garlic is golden brown.

Fish

Mamma Agata's Secret
Always add ingredients to room temperature extra virgin olive oil and cook from room temperature. This will help infuse the flavors into the oil.

Place the stuffed squid and the remaining half of the fresh chopped parsley (and any of the extra tentacle filling – if there is any) into the pan (9, 10). Sear the squid on all sides.

After the squid is seared, add the fresh tomato purée and oregano (11). Reduce the heat and simmer for thirty minutes.

Remove the pan from the stove, slice the squid into pinwheels about 1.5 cm or 1/2 inch wide (similar to a sushi roll), and serve hot, covering the squid with the tomato sauce.

Sauté di cozze e vongole
SAUTÉ OF MUSSELS AND CLAMS

Serves 4
500 gr (about 2 dozen fresh mussels in the shell)
500 gr (about 2 dozen fresh clams in the shell)
4 Tablespoons extra virgin olive oil
2 cloves garlic
1 Tablespoon fresh parsley (chopped)
A pinch black pepper
A pinch of salt
1 lemon

Wash and clean the mussels and clams.
In a non-stick pan (a Paella pan works well for this dish), heat the olive oil and cloves of garlic over medium heat and cook until the garlic is golden brown (1). NOTE: Do not burn the garlic or it will become bitter.

Mamma Agata's Secret
Always add ingredients to room temperature extra virgin olive oil and cook from room temperature. This will help infuse the flavors into the oil.

Add the mussels, clams, parsley and a pinch of salt to the pan (2). Stir the ingredients (3).
Cover and sauté the mussels and clams for a few minutes until the shells begin to open. IMPORTANT NOTE: Discard any clams or mussels that do not open!
Add a pinch of black pepper to the pan of mussel and clams.
Serve hot with lemon wedges, squeezing the lemons on top of the shellfish, as desired!

Alternative serving suggestion: If you wish to use them with pasta,
• Cook the pasta.
• Prepare the mussels and clams as above.
• Take the meat out of some of the clams and mussel shells.
• Add pasta to the clam and mussel meat, with their juice.
• Stir the pasta and cook for two minutes, to infuse the flavors.
• When serving, add a few of the mussels and clams in the shells as a garnish.
• NOTE: Mamma Agata would never top a fish dish with Parmigiano cheese and it will cover the freshness of the fish's flavor.

Impasto pizza
Pizza Dough

Serves 4
500 gr or 2 1/8 cup flour (Type "00" or white pastry)
15 gr or 1 teaspoon sugar
Pinch of Sea salt
4 Tablespoons extra virgin olive oil
25 gr or 1 ¾ Tablespoons dry yeast
125 ml or ½ cup lukewarm/tepid water
125 ml or ½ cup room-temperature milk

Mamma Agata's Secret
This process is simple, but needs to be done somewhat quickly. Mamma Agata adds the ingredients (such as olive oil and sugar) with one hand and dissolves the yeast into the tepid water/milk with the other hand. Just practice and have fun!

Dissolve the yeast in a bowl with the lukewarm/tepid water and milk. NOTE: DO NOT let this sit for more than 3 minutes before adding it to the flour.

Mamma Agata's Secret
It is important that the water/milk is not too hot nor too cold; either extreme temperature will only kill the active bacteria in the yeast and your dough will not rise.

Mamma Agata's Secret
The milk is a little Mamma Agata secret. It makes the dough very soft; you will love it. It can be replaced with tepid water, but the final dough will not be as delectable.

Place the flour on your workstation in a circular mound (1).

Mamma Agata's Secret
This is one recipe where it really can make a difference to use the type "00" flour. Please do your best to find it.

Add olive oil to the flour in a circular motion (1).
Sprinkle the sugar across the flour (1).

Add the water, milk and yeast mixture (2) and the salt into the dough and mix well using your hands (3). The dough needs to be moist and, above all, soft.

Mamma Agata's Secret
Do not overwork the dough or add too much flour. Both of these things will make the dough tougher.

Fold the dough towards you and knead it several times, just until the dough is uniform (4).

Place the pizza dough in a floured bowl and cover with a dry, clean towel. Let the dough rest for at least an hour to allow the dough to rise before preparation of your pizza.

Pizza margherita
Pizza with Basil, Tomato and Mozzarella

Serves 4
Mamma Agata's Pizza Dough
200 gr or 7 ounces fresh Mozzarella cheese – sliced
250 ml 1 Cup ***Mamma Agata's Tomato Sauce*** (see pag 55)
4 Tablespoons extra virgin olive oil (or butter or lard)
5 or 6 fresh basil leaves
Pinch of sea salt

Pre-heat the oven to 200-degrees Celsius (400-degrees Fahrenheit). Spread olive oil (or butter or lard) across a baking sheet or pizza pan with your fingertips (1).
Place the pizza dough into the middle of the pan and spread the dough to the edges of the baking sheet with your fingertips (2), until the entire surface of the tray is covered with dough as uniformly as possible.

Mamma Agata's Secrets
Wet your finger when you spread the dough so they do not stick while you are working with the dough.

Add ***Mamma Agata's Tomato Sauce*** to the top of the dough (3). Top the dough with the mozzarella cheese, a drizzle of olive oil (4), a few fresh basil leaves (5), and a pinch of salt.

Mamma Agata's Secrets
If your mozzarella cheese is in water, buy it two days before you want to make the pizza. Take the mozzarella cheese out of the water and place in a covered bowl in the refrigerator for two days to dry out (discarding the water). The excess water within the cheese will drain out and your pizza will not be soggy.

NOTE: If you like, you can also add a bit of oregano to the pizza for added flavor. However, the traditional Pizza Margherita does not call for it.

Bake in the preheated oven for fifteen to twenty minutes. Let the pizza sit for a couple of minutes (but not too long) before serving.

Pizza Fritta
Fried Pizza

Serves 4
Mamma Agata's Pizza Dough
250 ml or 1 cup **Mamma Agata's Tomato Sauce**
2-3 small zucchini (sliced)
2-3 eggplant (long, thin & firm is best)
2 sweet red bell peppers (small cubes)
1 litre or 1 quart peanut or vegetable oil for frying (NOTE: Do not use olive oil)
200 gr or 7 ounces fresh mozzarella cheese (small cubes)
100 gr or 1 lb bacon
1 small white onion (thinly sliced)
4 Tablespoons extra virgin olive oil
Sea sat

Prepare **Mamma Agata's Pizza Dough.**

Gather and prepare all your pizza toppings and the tomato sauce in advance (1).

Prepare **Mamma Agata's Tomato Sauce** (see page 55).

Slice the zucchini. Cut the peppers and eggplant into small bit-size cubes. Place them into separate colanders with salt to drain some of the water from the zucchini and peppers and the bitterness from the eggplant. Let them sit for five to ten minutes.

Follow **Mamma Agata's Frying Instructions** (see page 47) to fry the zucchini, peppers and eggplant in hot oil until they are golden brown.

Cut the mozzarella cheese into small bite-size cubes.
Slice the bacon in long, thin strips.
In a sauté pan, add the olive oil and onion. Cover the pan and cook on a low flame for five minutes. Remove from heat and set aside.

Take a small handful of dough and roll it into a ball; repeat this step until there is no more dough (1). Then stretch out the individual balls of dough into circles about 15 cm (6 inches) in diameter (2).

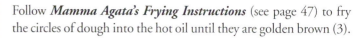

Follow **Mamma Agata's Frying Instructions** (see page 47) to fry the circles of dough into the hot oil until they are golden brown (3).

Remove the dough from the hot oil and add your ingredients immediately while the fried pizza dough is still hot, so it will melt the cheese and absorb the flavors of its ingredients. Always add **Mamma Agata's Tomato Sauce** first (unless you prefer a white/Bianca pizza), then the cheese and finally the toppings.

Here are some recommendations from Mamma Agata (4-10), include
1. Mamma Agata's Tomato Sauce, Mozzarella and Fresh Basil
2. Mamma Agata's Tomato Sauce, Mozzarella Eggplant, and Parmigiano Cheese
3. Mamma Agata's Tomato Sauce, Mozzarella, Bacon and Onions
4. Mamma Agata's Tomato Sauce, Mozzarella Peppers and Parmigiano Cheese
5. Zucchini and Smoked Provolone Cheese

Serve Pizza Fritta to your friends to create a memorable party that everyone will be sure to love!

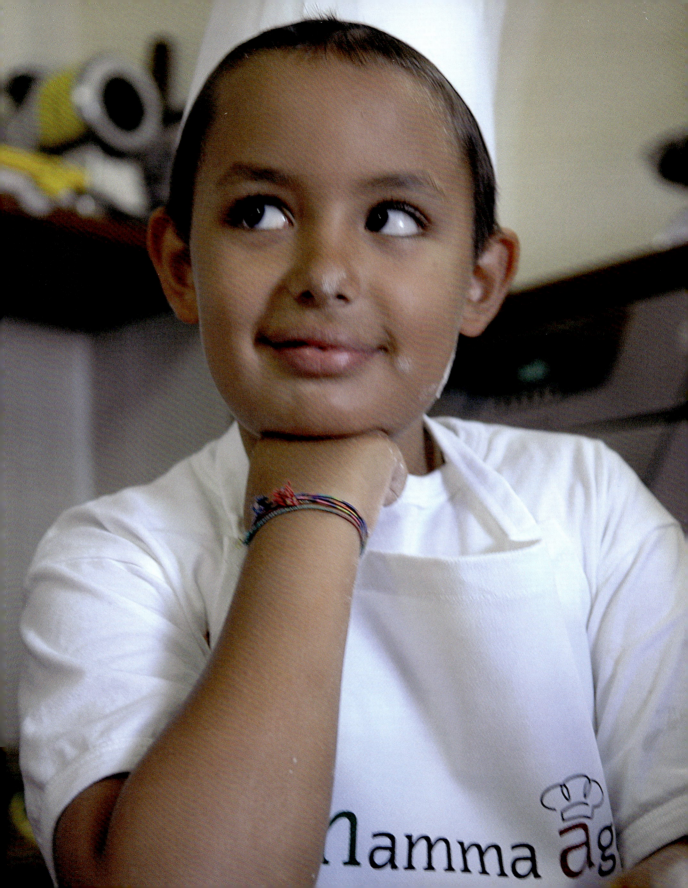

Meet Papà *Salvatore*

My mother and father met when Agata was only 14 years of age and married in 1964. Theirs is a true love story, beginning from the moment they first set eyes on each other that magical day when they met at Villa Civita, where Salvatore worked as a driver and a part-time gardener and Agata worked as a personal cook — they are living proof that there is such as thing as love at first sight!

Agata and Salvatore were married and remained employed at Villa Civita through the time my mother was pregnant with my sister Giovanna. Shortly thereafter, Salvatore left Villa Civita to begin a career as a waiter in a hotel restaurant and with much hard work and long hours, he became the Maitre d'hôtel and continued in this business for more than 40 years.

Salvatore's expertise in the hospitality industry provided our family with essential knowledge that was vital to opening a cooking school — he shared everything with us from showing us the proper way to set a table to the proper way to serve our guest and he even taught us some of the secrets in the hospitality business and the common mistakes to avoid. From day one, Salvatore has been the most amazing teacher and he continues to oversee each special occasion we host at the Hidden Treasure. You'll often see Salvatore walk up from the garden to the house and pass by the terrace and offer his advice on how to make the most of a table setting when we are preparing for a wedding, dinner party or other special event. We all love Papà Salvatore dearly, and we especially love learning new things from him every day!

What many of you may not know is that Papà Salvatore has a deep passion for nature. His love of organic food and animals is what provides him with the strength to work long, hard days in any type of weather, just so he can make sure that everything is just perfect for our family and our guests. In fact, all of the vegetables, including the tomatoes, peppers, eggplant, zucchini, herbs and fruit that Mamma Agata uses during her cooking class or for the special events are produced in the garden and cared for lovingly by Salvatore! His love and experience in growing organic vegetables and maintaining the grounds of the farm is also what helps us to prepare healthy and tasty dishes that are as fresh as you can get.

Meet papà Salvatore

When we say organic in Italy, of course we mean that no pesticides are ever used on our land and our vegetables are not genetically modified in any way. We do allow nature to help us out though, for example, our frogs and lizards eat the insects and protect the plants from harm, so we love the sound of frogs as we know they are busy protecting our precious vegetables!

Salvatore also plants the vegetables based on the cycles of the Moon, based on ancient theories of the effects of the Moon on our planet. He learned this precious information from his ancestors whose advice has been passed down through the generations and we can track it back on our property alone for more than 250 years!

For Papà Salvatore, the days in the garden are very long. Monday through Saturday, Salvatore wakes early and is in the garden by 7:30 am. He takes a short break for lunch and the heat of the day and returns to the garden around 3:30 pm and continues his work until 8 pm.
And just when you think Salvatore must be tired from all of the hard work in the garden, well, guess what? He also takes care of our animals, including chickens, rabbits, turkeys and ducks. There is no need to worry about my father though, as this is a labour of love, just like the work he does in the garden. Salvatore cares for the animals

as if they were his own children and Salvatore visits them twice a day to provide fresh water and he cleans their living space, and he also lets the hens out for a few hours each day to roam freely.

Mamma Agata loves her tomatoes, and so does everyone in the south of Italy; it is a staple in our Mediterranean lifestyle. Our garden grows 5 different varieties, and Salvatore plants each and every one of our Roma, Cherry, San Marzano, Grape and Sorrento tomatoes!

Each May, Salvatore plants the small tomato plants and once they reach a certain height, he builds a support system to keep the vines from touching the soil and dying. Tomato plants take a lot of water, so he must continuously water them so that they become delicious and plump, the exact way we enjoy in our cooking.

Every morning before the cooking class, Mamma Agata provides Salvatore with a list of what she needs, such as tomatoes, olive oil and herbs. Sweet Salvatore goes and gathers everything for her, just as she requested. Mamma Agata is also very sweet but is also very particular about her fresh and tasty ingredients. Papà Salvatore does his best to please her and all our students!

One of the most time-consuming tasks in the garden is caring for our precious lemon trees! They are very delicate and sensitive to cold weather, so when winter arrives, we must cover them with the green nets, you can see them scattered along the Amalfi Coast.

The nets are designed to protect the young lemons from the frost and in the summer we must remove the nets to uncover the lemons so they can enjoy in the summer sun and so that they do not become overly hot from the extra heat of the nets. This is such hard work that we must hire 5 additional people to help Salvatore with this process. And of course, the lemon trees also need to be cleaned and trimmed so that they grow evenly.

But the lemons like the tomatoes are so important for us; we cook and bake with them, but also make the famous limoncello and tasty marmalades – the tastiest marmalade you could ever imagine! We use the oranges in the same way, and we use the strawberries and all of the other fruits of the garden to make preserves too.

We also make olive oil, produced from our own olives that we collect by hand. It is the most delicious olive oil and enhances our dishes with such a special and "genuine" taste.

We can't forget the grapes! Salvatore works so hard to grow the grapes to just the right point and to a level that produces our high quality red wine "Sancti Medici", that he makes with Gennaro, my husband and sommelier. Last but certainly not least, is all the work he does to take care of the honeybees and the production of our organic honey.

The science of starting and maintaining a vegetable garden is so important, so rich and needs love, nurturing, passion, devotion – all of the skills that Papà Salvatore possesses and that are necessary to maintain our Hidden Treasure. He is the REAL TREASURE because his love and devotion makes it possible to serve the most genuine and tasty organic vegetables, fruits and herbs that allows Mamma Agata to prepare some incredible meals, preserves and liqueurs.

Thank you Salvatore, we love you!

Insalata mediterranea
Mediterranean Salad

Serves 4
1 head iceberg lettuce (roughly chopped)
½ head red lettuce (e.g. radicchio) (roughly chopped)
A combination of fresh seasonal colorful vegetables, such as:
- 2-6 tomatoes (cut into bite-size pieces) – such as Roma or Cherry
- 1 carrot (shaved)
- 1 bulb of fennel (shaved or thinly sliced)

20 fresh arugula leaves
1 cucumber (peeled and sliced)
2 sweet bell peppers (sliced/julienne) – such as red, yellow, and/or orange
2-10 mushrooms (sliced)
3 Tablespoons extra virgin olive oil
Juice of 1 lemon (or 1-2 teaspoons of vinegar, if your prefer)
2 pinches of Sea salt

Wash all of the vegetables well and cut them, as directed above (1). Add the vegetables to a large bowl (1).

THE DRESSING:
Add the following:
- pinch of sea salt (to taste) (1)
- drizzle of extra virgin olive oil (2)
- freshly squeezed lemon-juice or vinegar (3)

Mix the salad well and serve!

Mamma Agata's Secret
Mix the ingredients with clean hands to really incorporate all of the wonderful flavors of the fresh ingredients in the salad.

Insalata di 'peperoni' e melanzane
Oven Roasted Eggplant and Sweet Bell Pepper Salad

Serves 4
4 medium eggplants (long, thin, and firm)
4 large sweet bell peppers (such as red and/or yellow)
1 teaspoon dried oregano
A pinch Sea salt
2 cloves garlic (coarsely chopped)
5 leaves fresh basil (coarsely chopped)
5 Tablespoons extra virgin olive oil
Juice of 1 lemon

Pre-heat the oven to 160 degrees Celsius (350 degrees Fahrenheit).
Wash the peppers and eggplant, leaving the skin on the vegetables.

Mamma Agata's Secret
The best eggplant to use for this recipe is long, thin and firm in texture. Japanese eggplant works well. Ultimately, the shape, firmness and (low) water content impact the success of a good eggplant. Less water in the eggplant means more flavor in your dish!

Place the dry, clean, whole vegetables on a baking tray and into the pre-heated oven for ten minutes (1).
After the initial ten minutes, turn the peppers and eggplant over to expose the other side and bake for an additional ten minutes. Remove the vegetables from the oven.

Mamma Agata's Secret
Place the eggplant and peppers in a large paper bag after removing them from the oven. This steams the skin and makes them easier to peel.

When they are safe to handle, peel and slice the peppers and eggplants lengthwise into strips (2). Place the sliced peppers and eggplants on a serving dish and top with oregano, a pinch of salt, chopped garlic, fresh basil and a drizzle of olive oil (3).

Mamma Agata's Secret
When you eat this salad, a squeeze of lemon juice on the peppers makes them easier to digest.

Vegetables

Melanzane a Funghetto
Sautéed Eggplant with Cherry Tomatoes

Serves 4
4 medium eggplants (long, thin & firm is best)
4 Tablespoons extra virgin olive oil
20 cherry tomatoes (chopped in half)
1 clove garlic (thinly sliced)
5 basil leaves
1 Teaspoon dried oregano
1 litre or 1 quart peanut or vegetable oil for frying (NOTE: Do not use olive oil)

Mamma Agata's Secret
The best eggplant to use for this recipe is long, thin and firm in texture. Japanese eggplant works well. Ultimately, the shape, firmness and (low) water content impact the success of a good eggplant. Less water in the eggplant means more flavor in your dish!

Wash and remove the tops from the eggplants, leaving the skin intact. Cut into cubes (1) and add to a bowl and sprinkle with sea salt. Set aside for ten minutes to assist in draining out excess water and removing the bitter taste. After ten minutes, gently squeeze out excess water from the eggplant. NOTE: Do not rinse off the salt, as eggplants are like sponges and they will absorb the water.

Follow **Mamma Agata's Frying Instructions** (see page 47) to fry the cubes of eggplant in hot oil until they are golden brown (2). Remove the cubes of eggplant from the hot oil and drain them on a paper towel to absorb any excess oil.

In a non-stick pan, add the extra virgin olive oil and thinly-sliced garlic and cook until the garlic is golden brown.

Mamma Agata's Secret
Always add ingredients to room-temperature extra virgin olive oil and cook from room temperature. This will help infuse the flavors into the oil.
Add the cherry tomatoes (3), fresh basil and dry oregano (4). Co-

ver and cook over medium heat for five minutes.

Add the eggplant to the sauce (5). Cook uncovered for an additional five minutes, stirring occasionally.

Serve hot! This recipe makes a great side dish!

Serving Suggestions: This eggplant dish is fantastic over pasta, toasted bread, or as a pizza topping.

Patate con olio e prezzemolo
POTATOES IN OLIVE OIL AND PARSLEY

Serves 4
1 kg or 2 ¼ lbs small potatoes (Red potatoes work well in this dish)
1 Tablespoon fresh parsley (chopped)
6 Tablespoons extra virgin olive oil
1 teaspoon Sea salt

Wash and peel the potatoes. Cube the potatoes into bite-size pieces.

Cook the potatoes in salted boiling water for five to ten minutes.

When the potatoes are cooked, drain and place them on a serving dish (1).

Add the chopped parsley (1), olive oil (2), and salt.

Potatoes can be served hot or cold, as a side dish (2).

Alternative serving suggestion: Once the potatoes are cooked, let them cool to room temperature. Add tuna fish, mayonnaise and capers. Mix well. Refrigerate for an hour and serve fresh!

Zucchine alla scapece
ZUCCHINI SCAPECE STYLE

Serves 4
1 kg or 2 ¼ lbs zucchini (large)
2 Pinches Sea salt
3 cloves garlic (peeled)
10 fresh mint leaves
6 teaspoons white wine vinegar
1 litre or 1 quart peanut oil for frying (or vegetable oil, if nut allergies are present)

Mamma Agata's Secret
Large zucchini are better to use in this recipe, as they hold up better once they are fried.

Wash and cut the zucchini into 1 cm or 1/3 inch disks (approximate size). Place the zucchini into a bowl or colander (1) and sprinkle with sea salt. Let them sit for five minutes to drain some of the water from the zucchini. After five minutes, lightly pat the wet zucchini with a clean, dry paper towel to remove the excess moisture.

Mamma Agata's Secret
Adding salt to the zucchini removes excess moisture, providing better frying results.

Follow **Mamma Agata's Frying Instructions** (see page 47) to fry the zucchini by placing the zucchini discs into the hot oil all at once, along with the cloves of garlic (2).

Fry the zucchini until golden brown (3). Once brown, remove the zucchini from the hot oil and drain them on a paper towel to soak up the excess oil.

Remove the garlic from the oil and discard.

Place the zucchini on a serving plate and sprinkle it with fresh mint and vinegar.

VIP AT M

JOANNA KERNS
Cooking class with Mamma Agata on the 8th June 2009

JOANNE KERNS
tasting the Spaghetti of the farmer

Joanna Kerns
American actress and director, best known for her role as Maggie Seaver on the family situation comedy Growing Pains from 1985-1992.

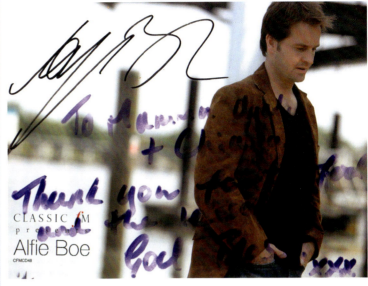

"What can I say about Mamma Agata's, The Hidden Treasure,......Heaven on earth!"
Alfie Boe xxx (Opera Singer)

"Thank you for the wonderful hospitality and education in authentic Italian cooking. It was a perfect end to a perfect holiday! I think we will have to come back!
Warmly, Dennis Franz"
(as Det. Andy Sipowicz in NYPD Blue)

Famous football players, Carlo Nash and Mark Schwarzer
(last two on the right) on the 31st of May, 2007.
Carlo Nash got married on the 2nd June;
this was his bachelor party arranged from Mark.

"Mamma Agata, Chiara and Gennaro
Thank you for a memorable...unbelievable... unforgettable night..."
Mark and Carlo Nash

Pierce Brosnan at mamma agata's cooking school on the 16th August 2009

Pierce Brosnan, his wife, Kelly, and their two sons, Paris and Dylan, are the most amazing people, so sweet and genuine.

I honestly was a bit nervous the days and moments before Pierce Brosnan and his family arrived at Mamma Agata's Hidden Treasure. I think that's normal when you start thinking, 'My GOD! I am going to meet 007!'

But the moment they walked in the door and I saw his children, his wonderful, beautiful and gracious wife, and the sincere smile of the handsom Pierce Brosnan, I just relaxed and my heart warmed up!!

We spent the most amazing day with Pierce Brosnan's family. After ten minutes, a HUGE bouquet of flowers arrived for Mamma Agata from Pierce and his family. Then, he came into the kitchen, cooked, took a lot of pictures and tasted all of our "simple and genuine ingredients" -- all home made.

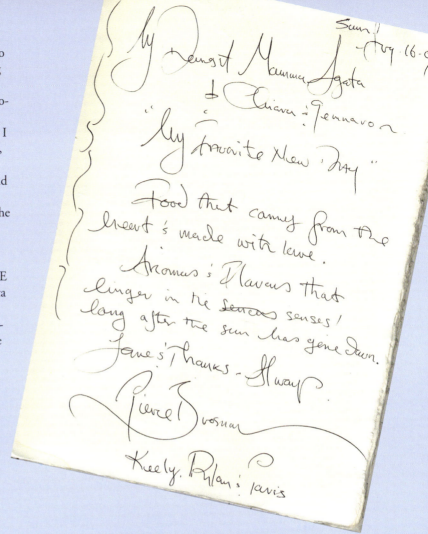

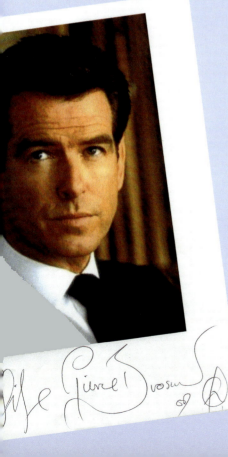

Later, they went into the garden to relax and to see our vegetables: the lemon trees, the herbs, and the flowers. On Pierce's return, he sat on our terrace and created the most wonderful painting for us. We cherish it and consider it a true HIDDEN TREASURE!

We sat on the terrace talking, laughing, and enjoying his website and the pictures from his films, life, and paintings. He explained to us how he did some scenes from his James Bond 007 action films. We spent such a wonderful afternoon together.

Keely, his wife, is the heart of the family. She cooks for them and she organised their amazing garden, planting bananas, mangos, and papayas. The family eats very healthy food and it is clear that they love each other.

I sincerely believe that Pierce Brosnan has a "pure and genuine Irish heart" and that love is spread to his wonderful family!

With love
Gennaro, Chiara, Mamma Agata and family

Dolce al limone di Mamma Agata
Mamma Agata's Lemon Cake

300 gr or 1 ¼ cups sugar
250 gr or 2 sticks butter (1/2 lb), PLUS an additional 1.5 Tablespoons butter, to grease the pan
4 eggs
Grated zest of 2 large lemons (4 lemons, if small)
A pinch Sea salt
300 gr or 2 cups "00" Flour
16 gr or 2 tablespoons of Pan degli Angeli Italian baking powder
125 ml or 1/2 cup whole milk
50 gr or ¼ cup hazelnuts (finely chopped and toasted)
Lemonade Mixture:
300 ml or 1 ¼ cups water
Juice of 3 lemons
8 Tablespoons sugar

Pre-heat the oven to 175 degrees Celsius or 350 degrees Fahrenheit. Whip the butter in a mixing bowl on high speed for at least two minutes (1).

Mamma Agata's Secret
Mamma Agata uses an electric mixer (with the rotating mixing bowl) for best results.

Add the sugar and continue to whip until a soft cream forms (1). Mix the baking powder into the flour and set aside.

Mamma Agata's Secret
Mamma Agata uses very fine flour (type "00" in Italy) for all of her recipes. Also, note that you do NOT need to sift type "00" flour.

Add the following ingredients to the mixing bowl, one at a time, and blend after each:
1. Eggs, one at a time
2. Salt
3. Grated lemon zest

Alternate adding and blending the following ingredients into the mixing bowl
4. Flour and baking powder mixture (2)
5. Milk (3)

In other words, add one quarter of the flour and blend; then, add one quarter of the milk and blend. Repeat this process until all of the flour and milk are blended into the batter.

Mix the ingredients on medium speed for about five minutes until the texture of the batter has a light and airy consistency (similar to a mousse). NOTE: Do not beat the batter for longer than five minutes after adding the baking powder.

Coat the surface of the fluted pan with butter (4) before dusting it with flour (5). Shake off any excess flour before adding your cake batter to the pan. NOTE: This step creates a non-stick surface so that the cake will easily release from the pan and retain its shape. Pour the batter into your greased and floured pan (6).

Mamma Agata's Secret
Mamma Agata uses a fluted Bundt pan for best results (6).

Bake the cake in the pre-heated oven for forty minutes at 175 degrees Celsius (350 degrees Fahrenheit).

Mamma Agata's Secret
Do not open the oven while the cake is baking or it will not rise properly.

While the cake is baking in the oven, prepare the lemonade mixture as follows:
1. Squeeze the lemons into a pitcher (or other container from which you can easily pour the lemonade mixture later).
2. Add the sugar to the lemon juice.
3. Mix until the sugar is fully dissolved in the lemon juice.
4. Add the water.

Once the lemon cake is finished baking, let it sit for two hours outside the oven to bring it to room temperature.

Mamma Agata's Secret
Now it is time to add the lemonade mixture to the cake – that is what makes it so moist (7/8).

Before we start this process, we want to ensure that the cake does NOT stick to the pan. In getting it to room temperature, the butter has solidified and that means there is a risk that the cake will stick to the pan. Here is the process just to ensure it does NOT stick to the pan before we proceed:

1. Place a plate on top of the pan.
2. Tip the pan over and carefully shake the cake out of the pan.
3. Immediately, place the cake pan back onto the cake
4. Carefully turn the pan back over.
5. Remove the plate to expose the cake.

This will seem like we have done nothing, but what we have done is to ensure that the cake will not stick later when we are ready to plate it.

NOTE: If the cake does seem like it wants to stick, you will need to place the cake back in the oven for a few minutes, just to warm the butter, and it will release from the pan easily.

When you pour the lemonade on the cake, there is a special process to ensure this is as effective and consistent as possible
1. Over thirty minutes: Slowly pour a little bit of the lemonade mixture all over the cake in the pan every ten minutes (i.e. three times in total). This will allow the cake to absorb the lemonade mixture very slowly. You should NOT have used all of the lemonade mixture at this point (7).
2. After thirty minutes, tip the lemon cake onto a serving plate (8) and add the remaining lemonade to the top of the cake, distributing it evenly all over the cake.
3. NOTE: If you feel that the cake is still too dry, you may make a little more of the lemonade.

Mamma Agata's Secret
We recommend this process so that when you flip the cake out of the pan onto a serving plate, the bottom will be just as moist as the top of the cake.

Garnish the cake with finely chopped hazelnuts (9) and enjoy!

Bogart and the LEMON CAKE

Mamma Agata had the pleasure of cooking for Humphrey Bogart and Lauren Bacall when Mr. Bogart shot a film in Ravello. He stayed in Villa Civita, where Mamma Agata cooked, for few days.

Mamma Agata always says that Humphrey Bogart was such an elegant man, who was incredibly handsome, sweet, quiet and who had a wonderful sense of humor.

In fact, it was Mr. Bogart himself that gave her the name "Baby Agata".

Mr. Bogart ("Bogey") was a peaceful man who enjoyed simple things in life. He loved to sit and relax with a good book while he was staying at the villa. He had one thing that he would not go without at any meal, whether it was breakfast, lunch or dinner - and that was the now-famous **Mamma Agata's Lemon Cake**, that he loved tremendously.

Mamma Agata (or Baby Agata, as he knew her at the time) adored Bogey just as much as he adored her cake!

Pasta Frolla

Mamma Agata's Pastry Dough

500 gr or 17 ½ oz flour "00" (or white pastry, if you cannot find type "00")
18 gr or 4 teaspoons baking powder
200 gr or 7 oz sugar
A pinch Sea salt
200 gr or 7 oz butter (softened to room temperature)
Zest of 1 lemon (grated)
4 eggs: 2 whole eggs PLUS 2 additional egg yolks

Mamma Agata's Secret
This is one recipe where it really can make a difference to use the type "00" flour. Please do your best to find it.

Place the flour in a circle on a large work surface, leaving a hole in the middle of the flour (1).

Add the baking powder, sugar, salt, room-temperature butter (separated into little bits) (2) and grated lemon zest to the flour (3).

Work the flour with your hands until all ingredients are incorporated (4).

Make another hole in the middle of the flour mixture.

Add the eggs and additional yolks (as above) (5).

GENTLY mix the dough with your hands (6), just enough to combine all of the ingredients (7).
NOTE: Do NOT over mix or the dough will be tough.

Mamma Agata's Secret
Never use a food processor for this recipe as it will overwork the dough, making it tough.

Cover the dough with cellophane and place it in the refrigerator overnight.

Mamma Agata's Secret
Prepare the pastry dough one day in advance of using it in a pie or tart recipe.

Once you have chilled your pastry dough, you can create tarts filled with your favorite ingredients. See **Mamma Agata's Apple Tart** recipe as a guideline for creating your favorite recipe with **Mamma Agata's pastry dough**.

Desserts

Crostata di mele
Mamma Agata's Apple Tart

Mamma Agata's Pastry Dough
2 apples (peeled, cored and sliced into thin wedges)
50 gr or 1 ¾ oz pine nuts
50 gr or 1 ¾ oz dried currants or raisins
Juice of 1 large lemon (2 lemons, if small)
Juice of 1 orange
50 gr or 3 ½ Tablespoons sugar
20 gr or ¼ cup chopped hazelnuts
20 gr or ¼ cup chocolate chips
1 teaspoon cinnamon
1.5 Tablespoons of butter to grease the baking pan
10 ladyfinger cookies or similar plain dry cookie

Prepare **Mamma Agata's Pastry Dough** and set aside.

Combine all above ingredients, except the lady finger cookies and butter, in a mixing bowl (1-4). Place the bowl in the refrigerator for about an hour.

Mamma Agata's Secret
Place the bowl of apple-filling ingredients in the refrigerator for an hour to allow the apples to absorb the juices of the other ingredients, enhancing the flavor of the apples.

About ten minutes before you remove the ingredients from the refrigerator, sprinkle flour on top of the work station (5).

Preheat the oven to 150 degrees Celsius (300 degrees Fahrenheit).

Roll out the pastry dough using a rolling pin (5) until the dough is about 1 cm or 1/3 inch thick (6).

Grease the bottom of the pie pan with butter and lightly dust with flour. Shake off excess flour and discard.

Place half of the pastry dough into the pie pan, making sure the entire bottom surface of the pie pan is covered with dough (7/8).

Trim the pastry dough around the top inside lip of the pie pan

Desserts

using a pastry wheel (or knife, if you don't have a pastry wheel), cutting off the top edge of the pastry dough from the rim of the pie pan (9).

Crumble the ladyfingers on top of the dough in the pie pan before the next step of adding in the filling from the mixing bowl (10).

Mamma Agata's Secret
The ladyfinger addition is a Mamma Agata secret. The cookies will absorb the juice of the apples, lemons and oranges and allow the crust to become nice and crisp.

Add the ingredients from the mixing bowl (i.e. the filling) into the pie pan (11).

Take the remaining pastry dough, roll and cut it into long strips, making sure that the strips are long enough to span the top of your pie pan. Place the strips in a basket weave design across the top of the tart ingredients (12).

Place the tart in the pre-heated oven for thirty minutes until the top of the pastry is a golden brown.
Serve warm, possibly with a scoop of vanilla ice cream!

Zeppole di Mamma Agata
Mamma Agata's Zeppole

850 gr or about 1 7/8 lb potatoes
125 ml ½ cup whole milk
150 gr or 10 ½ Tablespoons butter
50 gr or 3 ½ Tablespoons cake yeast (or substitute dry yeast)
1 kg or 2 ¼ lbs flour (Fine "00" or white pastry flour)
150 gr or 2/3 cup sugar
3 teaspoons cinnamon powder (for dough mixture)
2 Tablespoons baking powder
1 pinch Sea salt
1 teaspoon pure vanilla extract/essence
Finely grated zest of one lemon
6 eggs
1 litre or 1 quart peanut or vegetable oil for frying (NOTE: Do not use olive oil)
250 gr or 1 cup granulated sugar
2 teaspoons cinnamon powder (for sugar/cinnamon combination)

Prepare all of your ingredients to be able to make the dough quickly, including the potatoes (below), sugar, cinnamon, baking powder, sea salt, vanilla, lemon zest and eggs (1).
Put the butter and milk in a pan and set aside (to help the process go faster later).
Crack all of the eggs into a bowl.

Boil the potatoes in salted water until they are soft but not mushy. Remove the potatoes from the water and let them cool to the touch. Remove the skins from the potatoes and discard the skins. Set the potatoes aside (1).

Mamma Agata's Secret
Boil the potatoes with the skins on, starting in cold salted water and cooking for approximately fifty minutes. Let the potatoes cool before peeling them enhances and preserves the flavor of the potatoes.

On your workstation, create a circular mound of flour with a hole in the center of the mound.

Add sugar, cinnamon, baking powder, salt, and vanilla to the flour (2).

Add the lemon zest to the flour (3).

Desserts

Mix the ingredients together with your hands (4).
Once again, create a hole in the center of the mound (5).
Mash the meat of the potato with a potato masher or ricer and work the mashed potatoes into the flour mixture (5).

Heat the milk and butter that we put in the pan earlier over low heat just until the butter is melted (not too hot -- as too hot or too cold will kill the yeast).
Once the butter is melted, immediately remove the pan from the heat and let it return to a little warmer than room temperature, so the butter does not resolidify, but it is not too hot.

Dissolve the cake yeast into the milk and butter mixture.

Add the melted butter, milk and cake yeast to the flour and mix (6). Add the eggs (7). Mix and knead the dough for at least five minutes. See Mamma Agata's Secret below for additional help.

Mamma Agata's Secret
Starting from the center of the mound, with your hand, stir in a circle, incorporating the wet and dry ingredients into the circle (8).

As it is all incorporated, then start kneading the dough (9). Lift the dough and let it fall onto the worktop a couple of times to create a nice soft consistency.

Cut off a small amount of dough (10) and roll it into long sausage-like cylindrical shape (11), with a 2-3 cm (1 inch) diameter/width. NOTE: The width of the zeppole is what matters for frying. You may play with the length as desired.

Create circles with the individual pieces by marrying the ends of the dough (12).

Place the circles of dough on a floured tray and set aside. Allow the dough to rise for about an hour and a half (ninety minutes) before frying.

Mamma Agata's Secret
Place the dough in a nice, warm location (away from drafts and air conditioners) to allow the zeppole dough to rise.

Follow **Mamma Agata's Frying Instructions** (see page 47) to fry the zeppole in hot oil until golden brown (13).

While the dough is frying, combine the sugar and cinnamon in a bowl.

Once the zeppole are golden brown on both sides, remove them from the oil and quickly drain any excess oil from the dough. Dip the zeppole in the cinnamon sugar mixture immediately so that they will absorb the flavors of the topping (14).

Serve hot!

Limoncello
LEMON LIQUEUR

Zest of 6 or 7 large fresh organic lemons (or 10 small fresh organic lemons)
1 litre or quart of pure grain alcohol or vodka
1250 ml or 5 cups water
700 gr or 3 cups sugar
Large glass jar (large enough to hold the peeled lemon zest and alcohol)

Mamma Agata's Secret
The lemons used in this recipe must be fresh! Fresh lemon zest has a very intense taste. In addition, using just a couple of green (i.e. un-ripe) lemons works well in this recipe (if you are able to find them).

Peel the zest from the lemons with a vegetable peeler (1) and place them into a large glass jar (2).

Mamma Agata's Secret
Try to avoid the bitter white pith of the lemon skin (under the yellow zest) and get as much of the flavourful yellow zest as possible.

Add the alcohol to the jar with the lemon zest (2, 3).

Cover the glass jar with cellophane and store it in a cool place for 7 days.

On the sixth day
• Boil the water and add the sugar to the boiling water.
• Stir the sugar until it is fully dissolved in the water.
• Set the sugar syrup aside to let it cool overnight.

On the seventh day
• Strain the lemon peels from the alcohol and discard the peels (4, 5).

Limoncello

Seventh day (continued)

• Pour the sugar syrup into the glass jar with the alcohol and stir well (6).

Serve chilled (from the refrigerator or freezer)!

NOTE: This limoncello will keep for one to two years. Just store the limoncello in bottle(s) with a cap or cork in your bar or in the cellar. When you want to drink it, chill the limoncello in the refrigerator or freezer before serving!

Backstage at

The photographer Roberto Sammartini (Still life photographer) checking the images on the computer.

Roberto ironing the linen before photographing…

Michele Pappalardo (reportage photographer and recipe step) and Jacquie studying the recipes before starting to photograph the recipes and to properly write them in English.

Mamma Agata

Roberto reviewing the images.

Preparing for the next photograph and checking the set up.

Roberto and my daughter Paola, she loved to taking pictures with Roberto!

My daughter Paola behind the scenes.

Backstage at

Me and Laura Faust (Ciao Laura) checking text; Laura was an important assistant in creating the book – we worked closely on the recipes, text and wording for months we emailed back and forth from Nashville to Ravello - day and night!

The graphic artist Giulia (Giulia draft of the book…but with fun!

Laura checking the text once again…

Mamma Agata

...azing!) and me reviewing the entire

Gennaro, me, Giulia and Stephanie (she is American and helped to check the recipes too) all working together on the recipes and photographs.

Gennaro and Giulia studying the best image sequence...

Me, Giulia and Gennaro... laughing at the HARD work we were all doing...but so proud of it!

Ravello AN ELEGANT LADY THAT SITS ON TH

Ravello
Amalfi Coast • Italy

Once I had the pleasure to meet a famous journalist and provided him with a personal tour of the town of Ravello, including all of the hidden paths and winding side streets that make our village so special. We stopped on a panoramic terrace where we enjoyed the breathtaking view from atop of Ravello; during our break, the journalist said something very special that has always stuck with me: "Ravello seems like an elegant lady that sits on the top of the mountain and observes life as it passes by her."

The little town of Ravello is suspended between sea and sky and glows brightly from the luminosity of the blue water below and its mounds of plush gardens filled with vibrant, fragrant flowers. The fresh air is always welcome and abundant throughout the year and sparks new life in ones sense of wellness and when combined with the perfumes of the wild Mediterranean scrub, Ravello is a very unique and much sought after destination.

It is true that Ravello is a place of infinite wonders; the beautiful Cathedral, which was built in 1087 and it is located in the

main square of Ravello: Piazza del Vescovado. In the same piazza del Vescovado which the Cathedral overlooks, rises the plain entrance, of the magnificent Villa Rufolo. The Villa, whose original construction dates from 1200AD, belonged to the powerful Rufolo family and has become an international icon for Ravello.

Just 10 minutes from the center of Ravello there is another magnificent iconic beauty of Ravello; the extraordinary Villa Cimbrone with its wonderful Belvedere of Infinity and immense gardens rich of statues, temples, fountains, natural grottoes such as the Eva's grotto.

And last but not least, Ravello is the City of Music. From the early 1950s, Ravello has been the home of the famous and celebrated Wagnerian Music Festival that is held every year in July but today the city's concert season lasts year-round.

As you can tell, I personally consider Ravello to be the PEARL of the Amalfi Coast!

Mamma Agata

"I met the legendary Mamma Agata for a cooking lesson. The view was stupendous, the food and wine tasted wonderful and it was one of best afternoons I have ever spent."

David Bullard
Sunday Times Lifestyle

"There was one famous local many insisted I meet: Mamma Agata, once chef of Humphrey Bogart and Jaqueline Kennedy, who offers private cooking classes in her home. I met the embodiment of a true Italian mother. She whipped up countertops full of regional dishes, lemon chicken, penne all'arrabbiata etc. As I sat on her terrace, surrounded by lemon groves, Mamma delivered a never-ending stream of homemade dishes-so fresh, it was like eating the sun."

Nicole Alper
San Barbara Magazine

"I had the privilege of meeting Mamma Agata, one of Ravello's finest cooks, who now teaches cooking in her home. Mamma Agata is the sweetest woman I ever met and her dishes… uhhh… are the best a simplest food I have ever had. Mamma, thank you."

Arthur Schwartz
Hosts "Food Talk" a popular New York City-based, nationally syndicated radio show and author of the book "Naples at table"-Cooking in a small kitchen-Soup Suppers…

"You'll fall in love with Mamma Agata. She is a jewel. Mamma's Italian cuisine is wonderful, and her sauces are pure art…brilliant. Her cooking class should be on your "must do" list while in Italy, and is the perfect compliment for your wedding-related events."

Henrietta Morris
Editor In Chief Exquisite Bride

Ms. Amato, better known as "Mamma Agata", owner of this 13-years-old school has cooked for celebrities like Elizabeth Taylor, Jacqueline Kennedy etc… Her food is so simple and genuine… her kitchen and terrace have the most spectacular sea view Mamma Agata's cooking school is considered one of the Top Cooking School in Italy.

Jen Murphy
Food and Wine Magazine
Italy's Top Cooking School

If you would like to learn how to eat good food in Ravello visit Mamma Agata's cooking school… Her house, her vegetable garden, chicken runs and coops, and the shady terrace where you'll eat what you have cooked along with excellent good homemade wine from Gennaro (sommelier) are all beautifully set beneath a rocky outcrop and above the sea.

Lucy Hughes-Hallett
Condè Nast Traveller

Mamma Agata was the chef of many famous people such as Fred Astaire, Frank Sinatra… But It's not just her brush with stardom that makes Mamma Agata's cooking school one of the best of Its kind in Italy- it's also the fact that she specialises in the kind of unfussy, tasty recipes that you might actually want to make at home.

Lee Marshall
Sunday Times Uk

Indice

Windows in time...........7

Tribute to Chiara Lima...........8

The story of Mamma Agata's Life...........11

The cooking school...........21

The Hidden Treasure...........27

RECIPES

Cocktails
Pastella di Mamma Agata - *Batter for Dipping and Frying*...........32
Coccoli di Mamma Agata - *Mamma Agata's Coccoli*...........34

Starters
Involtini di melanzane - *Eggplant rolls*...........37
Fiori di zucchine imbottiti - *Stuffed Zucchini Flowers*...........40
Parmigiana di melanzane - *Eggplant Parmigiana*...........43
I segreti della frittura - *Mamma Agata's Frying Intruction*...........47

Conserva di pomodoro - *Mamma Agata's Tomatoes preserve*...........51
Salsa di pomodoro - *Mamma Agata's Tomatoes Sauce*...........55
Salsa con pomodorini freschi - *Mamma Agata's fresh cherry Tomato Sauce*...........59

Pasta
Gnocchi di Mamma Agata - *Mamma Agata's potato dumplings - The dough*...........63
Gnocchi alla sorrentina - *Gnocchi with tomatoes and mozzarella*...........66

Index

Gnocchi con carciofi e pomodori secchi - *Potato dumplings with sundried tomatoes and artichokes*......69
Pappardelle con peperoni e salsiccia - *Sausage and red pepper pasta*......73
Pasta con pomodoro e ricotta - *Pasta with tomato and ricotta cheese*......76
Pasta con broccoli e formaggio affumicato - *Broccoli and smoked cheese pasta*......79
Pasta con zucchine tradizionale - *Penne pasta with zucchini - traditional recipe*......82
Pasta con zucchine e panna - *Pasta with zucchini and crème fraîche*......84
Pasta con gamberi e zucchine - *Pasta with shrimp and zucchini*......86
Spaghetti del contadino - *Farmer's spaghetti*......89

Risotto
Base per risotto - *Basic preparation for risotto*......94
Risotto al limone - *Mamma Agata's lemon risotto*......96
Risotto con funghi e salsiccia - *Risotto with mushrooms and sausage*......98

Sommelier Gennaro Petti......103

Meat
Arrosto di maiale - *Roasted pork loin*......111
Arrosto di vitello - *Veal roast*......114
Coniglio con pomodoro e olive - *Mamma Agata's rabbit with tomato and olives*......116
Coniglio fritto - *Fried rabbit*......118
Pollo al limone - *Mamma Agata's famous lemon chicken*......121
Pollo alla cacciatora - *Hunter style chicken*......125
Polpette di Mamma Agata - *Mamma Agata's meatballs*......129
Polpette al pomodoro - *Meatballs in tomato sauce*......133
Spezzatino di carne con patate e carote - *Beef stew with potatoes and carrots*......136

Fish
Mamma Agata's fishing lesson......141
Pesce al forno del marinaio - *Fisherman's baked fish*......142
Pesce al gratin - *Baked fish with Italian breadcrumbs*......144
Totani e patate - *Squid with potatoes*......146

Index

Totani imbottiti - *Stuffed squid*...........149
Sauté di cozze e vongole - *Sauté of mussels and clams*...........152

Pizza
Impasto pizza - *Pizza dough*...........156
Pizza margherita - *Pizza with basil, tomato and mozzarella*...........158
Pizza fritta - *Fried pizza*...........161

Meet papà Salvatore...........165

Vegetables
Insalata mediterranea - *Mediterranean salad*...........170
Insalata di peperoni e melanzane - *Oven roasted eggplant and sweet bell pepper salad*...........172
Melanzane a funghetto - *Sautéed eggplant with cherry tomatoes*...........175
Patate con olio e prezzemolo - *Potatoes in olive oil and parsley*...........178
Zucchine alla scapece - *Zucchini scapece style*...........180

Vip at Mamma Agata...........184

Desserts
Dolce al limone di Mamma Agata - *Mamma Agata's lemon cake*...........189
Pasta frolla - *Mamma Agata's pastry dough*...........193
Crostata di mele - *Mamma Agata's apple tart*...........197
Zeppole di Mamma Agata - *Mamma Agata's zeppole*...........201

Limoncello - *Lemon liqueur*...........207

Backstage at Mamma Agata...........212

Ravello...........216

Mamma Agata's Cooking School
piazza S. Cosma, 9 - 84010 Ravello (SA) Italy
Ph. & Fax +39 089 857845
info@mammaagata.com - www.mammaagata.com